Tafari Makonnen School:

Inspiring Lives of Achievement

Since 1925

Contributors:

Bisrat Aklilu · Doug Eadie

Alem W. Mathias · Abebe Abraham Joteh

Tafari Makonnen School Alumni Association [TMSAA]

Tafari Makonnen School Alumni Association
2810 Georgia Avenue, NW
Washington, DC 20001

For more information about this book or to order additional copies, visit the TMSAA website: www.TMSAA.net or contact us at info@tmsaa.net.

ISBN: 979-8-9923987-1-7

Cover and interior book design by Van-garde Imagery

To past, present and future alumni,
whose lives of achievement are a testimonial to
Tafari Makonnen School's greatness.

Contents

Foreword
About This Book
Bisrat Aklilu, Contributor

—

Chapter One
TMS: An Educational Beacon for Ethiopia and the World
Doug Eadie, Contributor

—

Chapter Two
Lives of Achievement: Fifty Profiles
Alem W. Mathias, Contributor

—

Chapter Three
*Creation and Growth of the Tafari Makonnen School
Alumni Association (TMSAA):
Alumni Response to TMS Founder's Adera (Solemn Plea)*
Bisrat Aklilu, Contributor

—

Afterword
Whither the Tafari Makonnen School Alumni Association?
Abebe Abraham Joteh, Contributor

Foreword
About This Book

Bisrat Aklilu, Contributor
TMS Class of 1967
President of Tafari Makonnen School
Alumni Association (TMSAA)

Foreword

Tafari Makonnen School: Inspiring Lives of Achievement Since 1925 is a journey that began in the first quarter of the last century, when a visionary thirty-three-year-old Regent of the Ethiopian Crown, Ras Tafari Makonnen, decided to introduce and expand modern education in his ancient land. He was convinced that education would broaden the horizons of his countrymen and unite them to move forward towards modernity with a national purpose. As a prelude to his ambitious plan, he undertook a long, 140-day visit to major European capitals, accompanied by some members of the traditional nobility, to observe Europe's advancements in technology, education, and infrastructure. His hope for getting assistance from the European governments he visited to expand education in Ethiopia did not materialize. He returned to his country determined to open a school using his funds and the financial contribution of other officials who share his vision. Thus, on April 27, 1925, the Tafari Makonnen School (TMS) was born, and will soon celebrate its Centennial. It is a school that educated and inspired thousands of students from all over Ethiopia. Many are now living in Ethiopia and throughout the world leading "Lives of Achievement," which is the subject of this book.

While the Tafari Makonnen School Alumni Association (TMSAA) was very keen to have such a book written to commemorate the TMS Centennial, it was also aware that it is not a simple task that can be accomplished by just any writer. It requires a great lead author who knows TMS and its visionary founder, has emotional affection and connection to the school and to Ethiopia, and is well-versed in issues of governance and education.

These are some of the attributes that describe Doug Eadie, a Peace Corps Volunteer who taught at TMS from 1964-1967 (I was one of his students) and the contributor of Chapter One, "TMS: An Educational Beacon for Ethiopia and the World," which is the heart of this book. Today Doug is the President and CEO of Doug Eadie and Company. An educator, management advisor, and coach to several school boards and superintendents in the US, he has written more than twenty books on making boards and chief executives more effective in their leadership. Doug has a long and close association with TMSAA and TMS, having been a keynote speaker at the TMSAA General Assembly and having interviewed many TMS alumni for his blog "Entwined Lives: Working Together to Bring Emperor Haile Selassie I's Educational Vision to Life at Tafari Makonnen School." He contacted me in early 2024 to inform me of his decision to retire from his work as a nonprofit/public leadership consultant. I proposed to him that we do a book together about Tafari Makonnen School for its Centennial, which he readily and gladly accepted.

As a management consultant and experienced author, Doug immediately put together a road map to produce the TMS Centennial book. The TMSAA Board and TMS alumni we consulted enthusiastically supported the plan. A Leadership Team comprising the four contributors to this book — Doug Eadie; longtime TMSAA Board Vice President Alem Woldehawariat Mathias; and Abebe Abraham Joteh, founder of CMI Management — and I spearheaded the planning and execution of the project. One of the first tasks was to identify about thirty-five alumni, later expanded to fifty (forty-eight alumni and two TMS Deans), who are representative of TMS alumni across generations that Doug would interview one-to-one. I put together the alumni list from the TMSAA database that reflects the broad spectrum of alumni with TMS memory and personal stories, origin, gender, and year of graduation. Alem W. Mathias took responsibility for the management of these interviews, which she did superbly and allowed Doug to carry out a smooth ninety-minute interview with each alumna/alumnus.

A Steering Committee was established in July 2024 comprising Petros Aklilu, the Founding President of the then Tafari Makonnen School Alumni Association in North America (TMSAANA), the predecessor to the current global Tafari Makonnen School Alumni Association (TMSAA); Dr. Moges Gebremariam, a physician and noted scholar of Ethiopian history; Mrs. Azeb Asrat, the first female District Governor from Ethiopia of the Rotary District covering Eritrea, Ethiopia, Kenya, and South Sudan; and Professor Meskrem Taddesse, Associate Professor of

Business Administration and a former corporate executive. The Steering Committee reviewed and commented on the book's project thrust, structure, work plan, and alumni selected to be interviewed.

This book is divided into five major segments, including this Foreword, contributed by each of the four authors. Chapter One, "TMS: An Educational Beacon for Ethiopia and the World," by Doug Eadie, is the heart of the book. Using historical records Doug discusses the visionary critical role Ras Tafari Makonnen, and later as Emperor Haile Selassie, played in ensuring the proper functioning of the school. Combining this research with the personal accounts of alumni he interviewed, he masterfully presents "why Tafari Makonnen School has been an educational beacon for Ethiopia and the wider world for a century." He examines the "preeminent product of Tafari Makonnen School that has made it a gold-plated educational brand in Ethiopia and many other nations around the world: the tremendously high-achieving lives that its alumni have led over the past one hundred years." And he describes in detail the TMS "culture of excellence" that, along with its "holistic" philosophy have been key to TMS's effectiveness as an educational institution.

Chapter Two, "Lives of Achievement: Fifty Profiles," contributed by Alem W. Mathias, contains the profiles of the fifty Tafari Makonnen School alumni whom Doug interviewed. As she aptly writes, "Their stories and contributions reflect not only individual success but also the collective spirit of TMS, which inspires achievement across generations." She presents her own story of family upbringing, and early and later schooling leading to TMS, where she benefited from "holistic development" programs that went beyond academics and sports to a range of extracurricular activities. These engagements brought out TMS students' inner talents and creativity. TMS also instilled in the minds of its students the importance of community service and the need to think and care beyond oneself for others in need.

I contributed, in addition to this Foreword, Chapter Three, "The Creation and Growth of the Tafari Makonnen School Alumni Association (TMSAA): The Alumni Response to the TMS Founder's Adera (Solemn Plea)." It presents the efforts of a group of dedicated TMS alumni who formed the alumni association as a vehicle to help their former school in response to the "Adera" ("Solemn Plea") of Ras Tafari Makonnen, which has become TMSAA's guiding motto. It covers the major activities and accomplishments of the TMSAA over the years. It concludes with the key lessons and challenges faced by the TMSAA and likely to be faced by other alumni associations that have recently begun operation. As TMSAA expands globally and new members join the Board, it is essential to put on record and document the evolution, successes, and challenges of TMSAA. This section will also hopefully encourage alumni of other Ethiopian schools to establish alumni associations to promote a culture of giving back to one's school and community.

The Afterword "Whither the Tafari Makonnen School Alumni Association?" is contributed by Abebe Abraham Joteh. Reflecting on the growth and achievements of TMSAA, Abebe invites the many alumni who have not yet joined TMSAA to join with their alumni colleagues to connect and network and "continue this journey of service and growth, embracing the future while honoring the past." He identifies several strategic growth opportunities for TMSAA and reminds us: "As we celebrate 100 years of excellence, let us honor the past and embrace the future. By uniting us as a committed alumni network, we can ensure that TMS remains a beacon of leadership, integrity, and service for future generations."

TMSAA extends special thanks to Artist Dawit Fasil, who designed the TMSAANA and TMSAA logos, and to Artist Lulseged Retta, who designed the TMS Centennial logo. The two TMS alumni are among Ethiopia's outstanding contemporary painters.

After the completion of the book, which extensively describes the unyielding efforts of TMS alumni to restore the Tafari Makonnen School name under the leadership of the TMS 75th Anniversary Committee, the Tafari Makonnen School Alumni Association in North America (TMSAANA), and the current global Tafari Makonnen School Alumni Association (TMSAA), on 19 February 2025, the Addis Ababa City Council, chaired by Mayor Adanech Abebe, approved the renaming of the Entoto Polytechnic College (EPTC) as Tafari Makonnen Polytechnic College (TMPTC). As this is a historical book, the Entoto Polytechnic College name used in some sections of the book is retained for historical accuracy.

TMS alumni will joyfully celebrate the TMS Centennial throughout the week of 21 to 27 April 2025, happy the original Tafari Makonnen name used when it was inaugurated on 27 April 1925 has been restored.

Chapter One

TMS: An Educational Beacon for Ethiopia and the World

Doug Eadie, Contributor

TMS Teacher, 1964-1967

Founder/CEO, Doug Eadie & Company

TMS: An Educational Beacon for Ethiopia and the World

A Transformative Educational Institution

Since its founding in 1925 by then-Regent Ras Tafari Makonnen, who five years later was crowned Emperor Haile Selassie I, Tafari Makonnen School has been an extraordinarily high-impact educational institution, making a tremendous difference not only in Ethiopia but also in many nations around the world where its alumni have lived lives of tremendous achievement. Tafari Makonnen School has from its very beginning been a transformative, life-changing educational institution, producing graduates capable of capitalizing on opportunities to further their education,

Regent Ras Tafari Makonnen, TMS Founder

to build high-achieving careers in diverse fields, and to make powerful contributions to the quality of life in their communities.

In a very real sense this book is a heartfelt response to Regent Ras Tafari Makonnen's "Adera" (or "Solemn Plea") to TMS alumni in his April 27, 1925 inaugural address at Tafari Makonnen School:

> This school is an instrument which will operate on our country's behalf through the knowledge which God gives to each of you accord-

ing to your lot, once you have matured in wisdom and have become vigorous in intelligence. So I beg of you to help the school which nurtures you, gives you the food of knowledge: to see that it does not shrink but expands, that it does not fall but grows in strength.

Having spent three years (1964-1967) teaching ancient history and English in grades eight, nine, ten and eleven at Tafari Makonnen School and being keenly aware of this illustrious institution's stellar performance, I naturally anticipated that the fifty Tafari Makonnen alumni I interviewed for this chapter would for the most part respond positively to my queries relative to their Tafari Makonnen School experience. This was a gross understatement, as it turned out. Almost to a person the alumni I interviewed felt that their experience as TMS students was deeply satisfying and even life-changing, and decades after graduating their passionate commitment to TMS was palpable. There is no question that these alumni see TMS as the preeminent source — indeed the fountainhead — of their high-achieving lives.

Azeb Asrat Hailemariam (1973) spoke for many of my interviewees in telling me that "I am who I am today because of my parents and Tafari Makonnen School," as did Haile Assegide (1972): "TMS made me who I am as a successful businessman." Dr. Aklilu Habte (1950) summarized Tafari Makonnen School's impact on his life in

Dr. Hakim Workineh Eshete,
First TMS Superintendent

terms of his "first real contact with modern life." 1963 graduate Daniel Jote Mesfin told me that his "pivotal years" at TMS took him "into manhood like an airplane taking off." Almaz Demissie (1966) told me that she was a dramatically different person when graduating from TMS: able to think "more broadly"; "more self-confident"; and "more responsible, finishing what I start." Tesfaye Aklilu (1962) described his student years at TMS as an "unbelievable experience that made me whom I am," and Amha Mersie Hazen, who also graduated in 1969, testified that "in a nutshell" TMS gave him "self-confidence and a passion for learning" and spurred him to "strive for excellence and to be of service to others." Major Argaw Kabtamu (1958) informed me that anyone fortunate enough to graduate from TMS should "be grateful for their success in life." And Hilletework Mathias (1966) testified that the "high-quality education, morals, and discipline I gained at TMS became the cornerstones of my success later in life." These are a mere sampling of the appreciative encomiums Tafari Makonnen School received from the fifty alumni I interviewed. TMS has been, without question, an extraordinarily consequential institution in the lives of its graduates.

TMS Class of 1950

In the Beginning: His Imperial Majesty Emperor Haile Selassie I

Doug Eadie with the bust of
Ras Tafari Makonnen in the
TMS Administration Building, 2012

My goal in Chapter One is to explain why Tafari Makonnen School has been an educational beacon for Ethiopia and the wider world for a century. My starting point is necessarily His Imperial Majesty Emperor Haile Selassie I. His far-reaching educational vision was a driving force in Tafari Makonnen School's establishment a century ago, guiding its development as a stellar, world-class educational institution both before and after the Italian occupation of Ethiopia (1935-1941). Even today, long after the Emperor's death, his vision inspires and guides the institutional renaissance — the literal re-invention and updating of Tafari Makonnen School — that is well underway, under the leadership of EPTC former Dean Teshome Feissa and his successor Dean Abdulber Naser and with the enthusiastic support of the Tafari Makonnen School Alumni Association.

TMS's Pre-eminent Product: Alumni Lives of Achievement

I then turn to the preeminent "product" of Tafari Makonnen School that has made it a gold-plated educational brand in Ethiopia and many other nations around the world: the tremendously high-achieving lives that its alumni have led over the past one hundred years. These consequential lives in a very real sense are the ultimate return on the investment of time and treasure in Tafari Makonnen School over the course of a century. In Chapter Two, "Lives of Achievement: Fifty Profiles," readers will find professional profiles of the fifty high-achieving Tafari Makonnen School alumni whom I interviewed for this book — compiled by my co-contributor and esteemed colleague, Alem Woldehawariat Mathias (aka Alem W. Mathias).

The TMS Institutional Model

I next examine in detail the institutional model — the conceptual architecture, if you will, that has made Tafari Makonnen such an effective educational enterprise in terms of the high-achieving alumni it has produced. My examination begins with Emperor Haile Selassie's brilliant — and courageous — strategic decision after the Italian occupation to invite French-Canadian Jesuits to assist him in transforming his educational vision into concrete reality, building an institution to serve as a model for the expansion of elementary and secondary education throughout Ethiopia. I pay special attention to two key facets of the institutional model that the French-Canadian Jesuits designed for the Emperor: the Culture of Excellence permeating every facet of Tafari Makonnen School, consisting, most importantly of a focus on superb teaching; and a Holistic Educational Philosophy and Program replete with opportunities to learn and achieve outside of the formal classroom setting.

I close my Chapter One narrative on a personal note, sharing with readers the story of my coming to Tafari Makonnen School in 1964 and explaining why serving as one of the four contributors to the content making up this book has been a true labor of love. Three Appendices follow the Chapter One narrative:

Appendix A, "Tesfagiorgis' Story," recounting TMS alumnus Tesfagiorgis Wondimagegnehu's prison ordeal under the Derg

Appendix B, "More on Encouraging Creative Experiments," describing two innovative classroom initiatives carried out with French-Canadian Jesuit encouragement

Appendix C, "Abebe Abraham Joteh Reflects on His Scouting Experience," explaining why alumnus Abebe Abraham Joteh found Boy Scouting at TMS such a powerful character-building experience.

Drawing Heavily on One-on-One Alumni Interviews

My exploration of the key components of the educational model that has made Tafari Makonnen School an international educational powerhouse draws heavily on my one-on-one video interviews with the fifty alumni of Tafari Makonnen School whose profiles are featured in Chapter Two. Conducted via Zoom and lasting an average of 90 minutes each, these open-ended interviews asked interviewees how they came to be Tafari Makonnen students, what their transition to TMS was like, what they found most and least satisfying academically and socially as TMS students, what might have made their TMS experience richer and more beneficial, and the difference their TMS experience made in their lives over the long run, among other aspects of their Tafari Makonnen School experience.

Over the course of my interviews with hundreds of chief executive officers and members of their boards of directors over the past forty years as a leadership consultant, I have frequently encountered interviewees who resented having to take time from their busy schedules and who had obviously not spent much time thinking about the questions I would be asking. I have grown accustomed to having to prod interviewees to respond in detail to my questions. My interviews with the fifty TMS alumni whose professional profiles are featured in Chapter Two were a dramatic exception to the rule. No resistance had to be overcome; absolutely no prodding was needed.

The alumni I interviewed enthusiastically shared their TMS experience, and they could not have been better prepared to answer my questions. My challenge was not to fill ninety minutes. On the contrary, to a person interviewees were so passionate about their TMS experience that my falling hopelessly behind in my interview schedule was always a clear and present danger. Their enthusiasm was palpable, making the interview process uniquely pleasurable — and tremendously productive.

I must acknowledge the strong support I received during the interview process from my esteemed colleague and co-contributor Alem W. Mathias, who serves as Vice President of the Tafari Makonnen School Alumni Association Board of Directors. Alem scheduled — and when necessary re-scheduled — every interview that I conducted. Since my video interviews were conducted via Zoom, with interviewees in various locations in Ethiopia, the United States, and Europe, connection problems were not rare. Because of Alem, I led a charmed life as the interviewer, never worrying about inevitable irritating technical glitches, which Alem handled with her characteristic aplomb. I had all the fun, while Alem did all the really hard work, for which I owe her my sincere thanks and appreciation. If she were my student, and I her teacher, I would award her the highest possible grade in academia: AA+ With Distinction.

Educational Visionary and TMS Founding Father: His Imperial Majesty Emperor Haile Selassie I of Ethiopia

The Emperor's Passionate Belief in the Power of Education

In my over forty years as a consultant to hundreds of public elementary/secondary school districts of all shapes and sizes throughout the United States, I have never encountered a public educational institution whose development was guided by such an inspiring, ambitious, far-reaching vision as that of Emperor Haile Selassie's for Tafari Makonnen School. Tafari Makonnen School is a concrete manifestation of Emperor Haile Selassie I's passionate belief in the transformational power of education in Ethiopia. In *The Negus: The Life and Death of the Last King of Kings*, the historian Angelo Del Boca observes that "From the earliest years of his regency, Ras Tafari focused particular attention on the problems of education." Del Boca goes on to recount that in 1921 the Regent, "dipping into his own personal patrimony," purchased the first two printing machines in Ethiopia, which "he used to print a weekly newspaper, *Light and Peace*, a monthly, *The Light's Revealer*, and a considerable number of books, for the most part religious in nature, some of them with a preface by him."

In his *A Splash of Diamond*, Fr. Festo Mkenda, SJ, points out that "Haile Selassie's love for TMS and for education in general was also deeply patriotic. He was convinced that 'a nation is seen as highly possessed of works of civilization due to its heritages of refinement from past generations and not as a work accomplished in one generation,' and that 'such heritages demand countless sacrifices.' TMS was his personal effort to eliminate obstacles to such a glorious future by paving the way for succeeding generations of Ethiopians." In a 1948 address, the Emperor affirmed his faith in education as a nation-building tool: "In order to retain her proper and rightful place, Ethiopia's sole means is education, through which she will be able to assist herself, maintain her independence, take an active and important part in world affairs and be a benefit both to herself and others."

Serving as an outspoken champion for public education in the Empire of Ethiopia and founding Tafari Makonnen School as the centerpiece of his educational strategy required considerable courage, as the Emperor's 1950 address at the Silver Jubilee of Tafari Makonnen School's founding acknowledged:

> On this occasion when We celebrate the Silver Jubilee of the Tafari Makonnen School and recall the struggle We made to overcome the opposing internal political forces that We encountered at the time when, having the building completed, We were recruiting teachers and gathering students in order to get the work started, We thank Our God who helped Us to achieve Our aim.
>
> Ever since the day We were elected by God to be the leader of Our beloved Nation, Our wholehearted desire has been to expand education with which Our people will develop and guarantee their independence, and since Our accession to the power of leadership, We have put on this cause Our utmost efforts as much as events permitted. And this school the Silver Jubilee of which We are celebrating today, has rendered evident Our desire and effort.

Tafari Makonnen School as the Emperor's Model for Expanding Education in Ethiopia

There is no question that His Imperial Majesty envisioned his namesake institution as a model for the expansion of education throughout the Empire. How else to explain his intensive involvement in recruiting French-Canadian Jesuits, whom he determined were the finest educational administrators and faculty available, to serve as the designers of the post-Italian occupation Tafari Makonnen School and eventually its top administrators and academic unit heads? The Emperor was determined to turn the re-opened Tafari Makonnen School into a true comprehensive elementary/secondary institution and center of excellence, and the Jesuits who arrived at Tafari Makonnen enthusiastically embraced the Emperor's vision.

Tafari Makonnen School was from its founding intended to be a school that was representative of all of the Empire — a veritable "melting pot" drawing students from every part of the country, from every ethnic group, every religion, every social and economic class, speaking a variety of native languages. This was an integral part of the Emperor's original vision in 1925, when creating Tafari Makonnen School. Ato Emmanuel Abraham, who served Haile Selassie in a number of senior diplomatic posts and as Minister of Posts, Telegraphs, and Telephones, Minister of Communications, and Minister of Mines, in his *Reminiscences of My Life,* recounts how he serendipitously happened to come to Tafari Makonnen School as part of the Emperor's strategy for building an educational institution broadly representative of the rich mosaic that is Ethiopia:

> His Highness Ras Tafari Makonnen had opened on April 25,1925 a modern school, named 'Tafari Makonnen School.' His aim was that, besides the boys who lived in Addis Ababa, young people from all parts of Ethiopia should come and be given the benefit of modern education together. He therefore ordered a number of provincial governors to select and send school age youngsters to Addis Ababa. Dejach Habte Mariam was also instructed to send boys from Wollega (Ato Emmanuel's home province), and 23 boys were chosen from among those studying Amharic, French, and English. . . . Preparations were made for them to depart for Addis Ababa in September 1925, after Meskel.
>
> A few days before their departure, a woman whose son had been selected to go to Addis Ababa went to the governor's residence early one morning and shouted her appeal. The governor called her to his presence and asked her the reason. She replied that she had heard that he was sending her son to a foreign country and, since he was her only son, she was apprehensive he would die there (in those days people in Wollega considered Shoa a foreign country) . . . . My name was then included, and I thus obtained an unexpected chance of going to school in Addis Ababa.

The Emperor's Personal Project

Tafari Makonnen School was not only the Emperor's namesake and the concrete manifestation of his vision for the expansion of education in the Empire, but also the object of his affection and his close personal attention, especially before the Italian invasion and occupation and in the late 1940s and the 1950s. Ato Emmanuel Abraham was one of the first boarders at Tafari Makonnen soon after the school opened in 1925. In his *Reminiscences of My Life*, Ato Emmanuel charmingly describes those early days:

> At first all the meals were prepared and sent to us from the Heir Apparent's (Regent Ras Tafari Makonnen's) palace. Sweets which we called 'sugar' and cakes used to be sent regularly to the 'Wollega boys' by order of His Highness. As the number of the boarders grew. buildings were put up and workers employed for the preparation of food, and our meals were cooked in the school compound. Even then, on Thursday of every week, 'Our Lady Woizero Menen' (later Her Majesty the Empress) used to bring us specially cooked food and honey water. She would sit at the head of one of the tables and watch while we ate. The Prince (Regent Ras Tafari Makonnen) would drop in and move from table to table talking to some of the boys and encouraging us. In this way, both the Prince and the Princess took care of us like father and mother, and we pursued our studies in comfort with a sense of well-being.

The Emperor's intense personal interest in Tafari Makonnen School continued after the school was re-opened after the Italian occupation. Assefa Tsegaye (1951) recalls fond memories of the Emperor in his informal memoir:

> I vividly remember His Imperial Majesty visiting us during dinner time at least once a month, bringing with him loads of fruits for us. He was a father to us all. He loved us, cared for us, and gave us the opportunity to grow and define our share of the world for the betterment of self and country regardless of the social status we came from. Christmas was special. We marched to His Imperial Majesty's Palace led by a drum roll so as to wish him Happy Ghenna (Christmas). He

in turn gifted us each a sweater and panettone cake. I also remember that at the end of the school year those students who were in the top 3 in their class going to Menelik's Palace to receive their prizes from the hands of the Emperor. The prizes were books, special fountain pens, and watches.

Fr. Roland Turenne, SJ, recalls the Emperor's personal attention in his *Memoirs of a Former TMS Teacher*:

> I remember his visits to TMS, especially during Lent, when a pick-up full of fruit would follow his limousine and park discreetly on the other side of our residence, hidden from the school. After dinner, bananas and oranges would find their way to the refectory to the delight of the students.

Among the other alumni who shared memories of their personal contact with the Emperor, Tilahun Workeneh Eshetu (1959) recalled a particularly poignant encounter with Haile Selassie. After a student demonstration, His Imperial Majesty appeared at the end-of-day study hall to discuss his vision for Tafari Makonnen School as the educator of students from all over the Empire and to share how saddened he was by the behavior of the student demonstrators. And Taye Brook Zerihoun (1959) recounted his nerve-wracking encounter with the Emperor on one of his visits, which ended well. Having been questioned by the Emperor while standing by his desk in the study hall, Ato Taye, a bit shaken, inadvertently sat down on the Emperor's cloak as he walked away, bringing His Majesty to an abrupt halt. Ato Taye feared the worst as a couple of the Emperor's security guards rushed over, but the Emperor only waved them away with a smile.

The Emperor's Vision Lives On

There is good reason to believe that the Emperor envisioned Tafari Makonnen School graduates joining him as allies — as a formidable force — in carrying out his strategy for modernizing Ethiopia. Ironically, a number of Tafari Makonnen alumni, many as students at Haile Selassie I University, participated in demonstrations that played a part in the Emperor's overthrow in 1974. And, of course, the attempted coup d'etat of 1960, which was led by TMS alumnus General Mengistu Neway, commander of the Emperor's own Imperial Bodyguard, had already seriously weakened the Haile Selassie regime a decade before student demonstrations became widespread.

However, the Emperor's vision for Tafari Makonnen School — and for the spread of high-quality elementary/secondary education in Ethiopia — did not die with the Emperor's deposition and murder; nor was it extinguished during the Dark Age of Mengistu Haile Mariam and the Derg. That vision lives on, inspiring the renaissance of Tafari Makonnen School now underway, originally led by former Dean Teshome Feissa and carried on by his successor, Dean Abdulber Naser, with the enthusiastic support of the Tafari Makonnen School Alumni Association.

The Ultimate Measure of TMS's Impact: Alumni Lives of Achievement

About Assessing Institutional Effectiveness

How can we determine the effectiveness and productivity of an elementary/secondary educational institution or system? This is obviously a major question in many countries, in light of the tremendously important role education plays in economic and social development and of the fact that high-quality education is typically a major budget item at the national and provincial/state level. It is also quite difficult to answer and often heatedly debated. Why should we care? Principally, in my opinion, the question deserves serious attention because assessing a public elementary/secondary institution's (or system's) educational effectiveness and productivity is the only way to objectively determine the continuing financial investment that should be made in that educational institution or system.

Over the course of my forty years of work as an advisor to the boards and top executives of hundreds of public-school districts in the United States, I have learned that the most common assessments of an educational institution's productivity and effectiveness focus on the measurement of what I call "functional excellence" rather than on bottom-line impacts and outcomes. In other words, they focus on the means to achieve the ends desired, rather than on the ends themselves.

These common functional assessments consist of such indirect input measures as dollars budgeted for specific budget line-items, such as teacher salaries and fringe-benefits; class size (fewer students per class ensuring more individual attention from teachers), faculty educational credentials, institutional management capacity (e.g., governance, strategic planning, financial planning and management systems, discipline, etc.), technological resources (such as personal computers), curriculum design, the availability of student services such as career counseling, and the like. These indirect measures are certainly pertinent, but they tell less than half of the institutional performance "story." Another useful but limited and indirect measure of a public-school district's effectiveness widely employed in many countries, including Ethiopia, are standardized tests measuring student performance in, for example, mathematics and English. Typically prescribed by national and/or provincial/state educational departments, these tests are administered at particular points in a student's educational career and often govern access to higher levels of education and to particular institutions.

The Acid Test of Institutional Effectiveness: Direct Outcomes/Impacts

The acid test of the effectiveness of any public educational institution, including Tafari Makonnen School, has to do with its most powerful outcomes and impacts. These make up its ultimate "bottom line" — the fundamental return on the investment, largely financial, in the institution. Without question, the most important and fundamental outcomes are changed lives — specifically, graduates capable of capitalizing on opportunities to further their education, to build high-achieving careers in diverse fields, and to powerfully contribute to quality of life — in their communities, nationwide and beyond. Tafari Makonnen School has passed this fundamental test of institutional effectiveness with flying colors, becoming early in its proud history an extraordinarily high-impact educational institution by this fundamental measure, in public and nonprofit management, for-profit business, the fine and performing arts, higher education — as faculty members and administrators — scientific research, medicine, international relations and economic development, law, and more.

A Note on Indirect but Important Outcomes

It is widely believed that high-quality public elementary/secondary education is a major factor in economic growth (an indirect outcome) — at the national, provincial/state, and local levels — in terms both of attracting business enterprises (whose employees' children benefit from high-quality educational institutions) and providing skilled workers for new and growing enterprises. The alumni of high-quality public educational institutions, many believe, also include entrepreneurs who invent new enterprises. It is also widely believed (certainly this was the opinion of Emperor Haile Selassie) that high-quality public elementary/secondary schools are a powerful nation building/patriotic tool, in the sense that their curriculums can include history courses that foster national pride and social science courses that foster responsible citizenship (for example, volunteering to assist in delivering social services). These beliefs tend to be intuitive, rather than research-based, so very often the actual outcomes fall significantly short of expectations, at worst being classical cases of what we call wishful thinking.

TMS Alumni Living Lives of Achievement

The lives of achievement generated by Tafari Makonnen over the past century have enriched and strengthened communities not only in Ethiopia, but in countries throughout the world. In this sense, Tafari Makonnen School has been an international educational powerhouse and model for elementary/secondary school design around the world. Here are but a few examples of high-achieving alumni lives made possible by Tafari Makonnen school (see Chapter Two for fifty detailed alumni profiles):

- Dr. Aklilu Habte (1950), after earning bachelor's, master's and PhD degrees from the University College of Addis Ababa, the University of Manitoba, and Ohio State University, served as a lecturer, department head, dean, associate academic vice president and president of Haile Selassie I University. He later held the post of Minister of Culture, Sports and Youth Affairs in the Government of Ethiopia and served as Director of the Education and Training Department and special advisor in human resource development to the Vice President of the Africa Region at the World Bank. Before his retirement, Dr. Aklilu served as Chief of the Education Division and Special Advisor to the Executive Director at UNICEF.

- Dr. Adam Abdallah (1960) earned his B.A. degree from the University College of Addis Ababa in 1957 and his M.S. degree from Boston College, after which he served in Ethiopia as a faculty member at the Harar Teacher Training Institute, Director of the Prince Makonnen Haile Selassie Secondary School in Dire Dawa, Director of the Harar Teacher Training Institute, Director

General of Secondary Education in the Ethiopian Government Ministry of Education, and Director of Ethiopian Secondary School Leaving Certificate Examinations. Re-locating to the United States in 1973, he earned his PhD at the University of Wisconsin, after which he held executive and teaching positions at Marquette University and the City University of New York.

- Addis Anteneh Kassa(1955), after earning his B.A. degree at the University College of Addis Ababa and his M.S. degree from the University of Illinois at Champaign-Urbana, held a number of positions in the Government of Ethiopia, including: economist in the Blue Nile Survey, Ministry of Public Works; Economic Studies Section Head, Ministry of National Community Development; and Head, Planning Unit, Awash Valley Development Authority. He later served as Chairman of the Board of Directors of the Bank of Abyssinia.

- Major Argaw Kabtamu (1958) graduated from the Haile Selassie I Military Academy at Harar with the rank of Second Lieutenant, after which he served as an instructor at the Academy for five years. His subsequent career included serving as Aid to the Ethiopian Army Deputy Chief of Staff Major General Assefa Ayene, Head of Training at the Army Headquarters, and as security representative of Ethiopian Airlines at the Paris Airport, and a second tour of duty as an instructor at the Harar Military Academy. He later served as First Secretary, Counsellor, and acting Chargé d'affaires in the Ethiopian Ministry of Foreign Affairs.

- Petros Aklilu (1966) completed three years at Haile Selassie I University before receiving his BS degree in economics from Oklahoma State University and his MS degree in agricultural economics from the University of Massachusetts. Petros, after a stint at the Awash Valley Authority in Addis Ababa as a planning/project economist, began a long, distinguished career at the World Bank. His many positions at Bank before his retirement in 2007 included Economist, Agriculture Division; Senior Economist, Irrigation Division and Agriculture Operations Division; Head of Operations, Resident Mission: Pakistan; Sector Leader, Rural Development, Water and Environmental Group; and Chief, Economic Analysis and Development Policy Unit.

- Professor Meskerem Tadesse (1968) was awarded BS and MBA degrees from the University of Pittsburgh in the United States. After serving in senior executive positions at the Mobay Chemical Corporation and the Chrysler Corporation, she founded a high-end Ethiopian boutique, Meski's Modes Internationale, in Greektown, Michigan. She is currently a tenured associate professor of business administration at the University of the West in Rosemead, California and Director of the Center for Minority and Small Business and Editor, "Minority & Small Business Review." She also served as Co-Chair of the California Governor's Conference on Small Business and as a visiting professor at St. Mary's University in Addis Ababa.

- Azeb Asrat Hailemariam (1973) earned her BS degree at Addis Ababa University, after which she began a 28-year career in the United Nations World Food Program, holding a number of senior leadership positions, including Project Officer in Ethiopia, Emergency Coordinator in Bosnia Hercegovina, Regional Program Coordinator for South East Asian Countries, Senior Regional Program Advisor for East, Central and Southern African Countries, and Deputy Country Director in Sri Lanka and Sudan. Her United Nations career has been followed by an illustrious volunteer career with Rotary, including serving as District Governor covering Eritrea, Ethiopia, Kenya and South Sudan.

Lives of Achievement Disrupted and Ended Under the Derg

"I am living now at peace — of course, doing everything I can to forget my dark days." These are Tesfagiorgis Wondimagegnehu's closing words in the video we had just filmed in my room at the Jupiter International Hotel in Addis Ababa the last morning of my ten-day return visit to Ethiopia in May 2012. Sitting across from Tesfagiorgis (a 1968 TMS graduate), keeping my eye on the camera as he told the story of his experience in the late 1970s under the military group — the Derg — that had overthrown Emperor Haile Selassie, I now understood fully how terribly dark those days were for my Ethiopian friend. And I realized what a miracle it was that Tesfagiorgis was alive and well — happily married to Almaz with two beautiful children, Bersabel and Natnael — and that we were together again almost a half-century after saying goodbye at Bole International Airport when I returned to the States from Ethiopia in 1967.

Tesfagiorgis and Doug at the Institute of Ethiopian Studies, 2012

The majority of Tafari Makonnen School alumni whose lives of achievement are described in this book pursued their careers largely outside of Ethiopia, principally in the United States, because their lives were endangered and/or their professional opportunities were so severely limited during the dark period under Mengistu Haile Mariam and the Derg. Some were able to remain in Ethiopia and pursue their careers without major disruption during this period (1974-1991). But many Tafari Makonnen School alumni were murdered under the Derg, or, like Tesfagiorgis, had their lives severely disrupted by imprisonment. Tesfagiorgis survived and managed to live a life of significant achievement. You will find the detailed account of his experience under the Derg in Appendix A, "Tesfagiorgis' Story."

Bringing Emperor Haile Selassie's Vision to Life: Creating a Magical, World-Class Educational Institution

Seeking the Keys to the Magic

Not long after I arrived in Addis Ababa in early September 1964 and settled into my temporary home in a dormitory at Empress Menen School, along with several other Peace Corps teachers assigned to the capital city, I learned from Ethiopia Peace Corps headquarters that I would be teaching at Tafari Makonnen School. Although aware that "Tafari Makonnen" was Emperor Haile Selassie's pre-coronation name, I knew absolutely nothing about the school, and in those days Googling "TMS" was not possible. A week or so after receiving my assignment and renting a house facing the front gate of Empress Menen School along with two other Peace Corps Volunteers assigned to Tafari Makonnen School, Garber Davidson and Randy Sword, I finally visited the school where I would spend the next three years.

Walking through the front gate and down the road to the iconic administration building of Tafari Makonnen School for my meeting with the academic head, Mr. Marcel Gareau (I had no idea he was a Roman Catholic priest), for my initial orientation and teaching assignments, I realized that I would be joining a "major league" institution, many times larger than the secondary school I had graduated from in the States. The sheer size of the campus, with its various classroom buildings, in-

Flower Garden in Front of the TMS Administration Building

cluding the imposing four-story building housing the Commercial Section classrooms, the large library a few steps away, and several well-groomed athletic fields, had the feel of a medium-size college rather than a public elementary/secondary school.

Mr. Gareau must have provided me with an overview of the school, but I cannot recall the details of his orientation that day almost sixty years ago. What I do remember vividly is our discussion after he informed me that I would, in addition to several tenth grade English classes, be teaching ninth-grade ancient history. Although I majored in history at the University of Illinois, I protested, I had not taken even one ancient history course. Smiling, he suggested that I get busy reading in the specific areas I would be covering — Greece, Rome, Egypt and Mesopotamia — during lunch breaks, evenings, and weekends, as well as during the winter break. He suggested that I borrow standard ancient history texts from the Haile Selassie I University library and offered to share resource material in his voluminous files, including, I recall, several National Geographic pieces on ancient Egypt. His positive, can-do attitude and faith in the inexperienced twenty-two-year-old he was meeting with were energizing and gave me an inkling of the very special institution I would soon be joining.

When I returned to the US in June 1967, I well knew that Tafari Makonnen School was a magical place to learn and to practice the fine art of teaching. I had loved every minute I spent in the classroom, and had come to respect, admire, and feel deep affection for the hundreds of students I had taught. But I did not really understand at that point what made Tafari Makonnen School such an amazing — indeed, magical — educational institution. I was a classroom teacher,

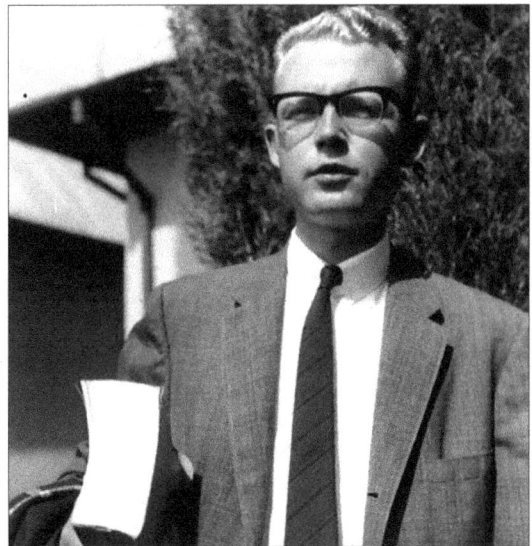

Doug Outside Classroom:
First Day of Class, 1964

not a student of institutional development. Fuller understanding came only years later, after I had earned my Master of Management Science degree at Case Western

Reserve University, had founded my own consulting firm specializing in nonprofit and public chief executive and board leadership, and had worked with over a hundred public school systems of all shapes and sizes throughout the United States. Now I was prepared to see Tafari Makonnen School through a far different lens in search of the keys to its institutional magic, and co-authoring this book has provided the opportunity to examine these keys.

The Critical Nexus of Vision and Strategy

This chapter has already paid considerable attention to His Imperial Majesty Emperor Haile Selassie's inspiring, far-sighted vision that guided the establishment of Tafari Makonnen School in 1925, and the tenacity and courage that enabled the Emperor to neutralize, if not eliminate, the widespread opposition among members of the aristocracy and leaders of the Ethiopian Orthodox Church to expanding modern elementary/secondary education in Ethiopia. After the Italian occupation was ended in 1941, the Emperor, as Fr. Festo Mkenda, SJ, points out in his *A Splash of Diamond*, "had to deal with the fresh problem of rebuilding his school from the ruins that the Italians had left behind."

Haile Selassie's brilliant solution — inviting French-Canadian Jesuits to take hands-on charge of making TMS, in Fr. Festo's words, "the first quintessentially model school in the country" — created the critical nexus between aspirational vision and the concrete, hands-on strategy that is essential for realizing a vision in practice. Haile Selassie recognized that his vision, no matter how far-sighted and inspiring, could not alone turn Tafari Makonnen School into the national educational model he envisioned. He needed primary/secondary education experts with a solid track record in institutional planning and management systems development, in day-to-day nuts and bolts administration, and in classroom teaching to take the lead in TMS's institutional development, and the French-Canadian Jesuits perfectly fit the bill.

In *A Splash of* Diamond, Fr. Festo Mkenda, SJ, describes how the French-Canadian Jesuits, masters of the art of educational institution building, went about transforming Tafari Makonnen School into a modern, comprehensive elementary/secondary educational institution: systematically growing student enrollment; expanding faculty; making significant capital improvements, such as the new four-story building that originally housed student dormitories, a kitchen and dining hall and eventually classrooms in the school's Commercial Section, and a number of new playing fields; designing a modern academic curriculum not only geared toward preparing students for post-secondary education, but also offering practical shop courses focused on manual skills, and setting clear academic standards; upgrading instruction through systematic guidance and supervision, monthly tests and report cards, and end-of-year examinations; holding regular staff meetings; and the like.

The remainder of this chapter will focus on two critical building blocks of the Tafari Makonnen School Institutional Model that the French-Canadian Jesuits designed — within the framework of Emperor Haile Selassie's vision — that have made Tafari Makonnen School a truly unique, tremendously high-impact educational institution and a global educational beacon and brand: the TMS *Culture of Excellence* and its rich *Extracurricular Program mirroring the Jesuit Holistic Educational Philosophy*.

The Tafari Makonnen School Culture of Excellence

The Meaning of Culture

"Organizational culture" is a rather nebulous concept, as our readers are no doubt aware. My working definition of the term is simple: the internal milieu of a particular organization — ranging from a whole nation to a particular local organization such as Tafari Makonnen School — characterized by shared values, beliefs, principles, practices and even feelings. The first time I can recall thinking about Tafari Makonnen School in terms of a unique culture was the summer of 1967 after returning to the United States from Ethiopia. That summer I was seriously considering graduate fellowship offers from a number of universities and one highly selective liberal arts college: Oberlin, in Ohio not far from Cleveland. At that time the need for public school teachers was acute around the United States, and Oberlin was offering a new, one-year Master of Arts in Teaching degree aimed at people like me with a BA degree but no formal teacher training, much less certification.

Since I had loved teaching at Tafari Makonnen School, I was initially more than a little interested in Oberlin's offer. What led me to accept the offer of Case Western Reserve University's School of Management instead was primarily my "gut" feeling, on reflection, that the likelihood of my finding a teaching position in an American public secondary school that would provide me with the deep satisfaction I had experienced at Tafari Makonnen School was virtually nil. Of course, I might have been wrong, but meetings that summer with administrators from two well-regarded public-school districts reinforced my initial feeling. I was not fully aware at the time, but what I think I most feared was working in a public school district lacking what I have come to think of as Tafari Makonnen School's "Culture of Excellence." Allow me to explain what the concept meant — and means — to me, from my perspective as a former Tafari Makonnen School faculty member.

Pride

A striking element of Tafari Makonnen's Culture of Excellence was the palpable pride that TMS administrators, faculty, and students felt at being part of Emperor Haile Selassie's school — his namesake, his personal project, the object of his intense personal attention and, most important, the model he intended to employ in expanding educational opportunities throughout the nation. On many occasions since he had founded Tafari Makonnen School in 1925, the Emperor made clear that Tafari Makonnen was so much more than a comprehensive, modern elementary/secondary educational institution located in Ethiopia's capital city. It was the embodiment of his passionate belief that education was the key to transforming Ethiopia into a modern nation and a key element of his strategy for carrying out this transformation. The faculty colleagues and students I worked with during my three-year "tour of duty" at Tafari Makonnen School well understood — and took great pride in — being part of His Imperial Majesty's grand, transformative and patriotic educational mission.

To be sure, the Derg succeeded in dismantling the ancient monarchy and eliminating many physical traces of the Emperor throughout Ethiopia during its almost twenty years in power. But I am confident that, as the renaissance of Tafari Makonnen School now underway — originally under the leadership of former Dean Teshome Feissa and now under his successor Dean Abdulber's leadership and with TMSAA's strong support — moves forward, the Emperor will receive the credit he deserves — not only for founding and nurturing Tafari Makonnen School — but also for making the school a key part of his strategy for expanding education throughout his Empire.

The great majority of alumni I interviewed for this book made a special point of mentioning two other features of Tafari Makonnen School that strengthened their feelings of pride: the school's reputation for high academic standards and stellar academic performance; and its handsome and well-maintained campus. The physical plant of Tafari Makonnen School radiated excellence. The handsomely stocked library, which students were encouraged to use, would be the envy of any public school district anywhere, including the United States (Having served as president of the Librarians Club of the secondary school I attended in Illinois, I can attest to my high school library's being distinctly inferior to Tafari Makonnen School's). The classroom buildings were well-maintained, and the classrooms well-equipped. Science classes benefitted from superbly equipped laboratories, which many alumni remembered using after class hours at the invitation of their teachers. Even the several large playing fields were kept in immaculate condition. I know from personal experience that you could not walk far on the Tafari Makonnen campus without, as I wrote earlier in this chapter, feeling that you were in a truly "major league" institution — the product of careful design and meticulous care.

TMS Chemistry Lab, 1949. (Courtesy of Assesfa Tsegaye , class of 1951)

Highly Effective Teaching

At the heart of Tafari Makonnen School's Culture of Excellence is, of course, highly effective teaching. Every one of the fifty alumni I interviewed for this book cited top-quality teaching as a preeminent reason why their Tafari Makonnen experience was so satisfying, and ultimately so beneficial for their careers. For example, Yilma Kassaye (1962) described his academic experience as "fantastic," characterized by "superb" teaching that made lessons "come alive." Fikre Mariam Tsehai (1967) cited both "excellent" and "caring" teachers. Merafe Seyoum (1968) found her teachers "very caring and helpful." Tadesse Goshime (1969) testified that his teachers were always "well-prepared" and "demanding" in class. Selamawit Yissma (1971) credited her teachers with strengthening her "critical thinking." Bahrnegash Bellete (1971) described his teachers as "making the curriculum come to life" and as "supportive" and "caring." Getachew Tesfaye (1973) cited "really quality teaching" and "individual attention." Dr. Mohammed Sherif (1974) described his teachers as "highly qualified" and "passionate." Getaw Worku Hassen (1987) appreciated that his teachers explained "complex" matters "simply," made time for class discussion, and buttressed students' self-confidence by having them stand at the blackboard and solve problems before the whole class.

Taking a Personal Interest in Students

In addition to their excellent work in the classroom, Tafari Makonnen teachers took a personal interest in their students, paying close attention not only to their classroom experience, but also to their lives outside the classroom. This was especially the case when girls joined TMS's Commercial Section not long after its establishment. Konjit Tedla (1973), saying that she suffered more than a little "culture shock" when transferring to TMS, testified that the welcome party hosted by Commercial Section students and teachers eased her transition to a radically different milieu. And Almaz Demissie (1966) shared a charming story demonstrating the "human" side of Tafari Makonnen administrators and teachers in my interview with her. Walking down the street near the school one day, she was hailed by the second-in-command, Assistant Director Gerard Gagnon, who was driving by. He stopped to chat, and learning that her home was close-by, he asked if he could give her a lift home. When they arrived, he accepted her invitation to come inside and eat freshly made injera.

10th-Grade English Class

Relative to taking a personal interest in the lives of students, the custom while I was teaching at Tafari Makonnen School was for the school's director or assistant director (I cannot now, sixty years later, recall which) to ask Peace Corps teachers at TMS to provide selected needy students with sleeping space in their homes and meals. All of my three years at Tafari Makonnen School, my housemates and I hosted students — a total of six or seven if memory serves me well — in our home. My housemates and I benefitted from the arrangement in two important ways: gaining a deeper understanding of our Ethiopian students and their cultural backgrounds; and forming strong personal relationships with at least some of our "boarders." I, for example, felt that the two students who were living with me when I completed my tour of duty at Tafari Makonnen School, Tesfagiorgis Wondimagegnehu and Tariku Belay, were like younger brothers, and one of the great joys of my post-Tafari Makonnen School life has been to reunite with both of them a half-century after returning to the United States.

The Multi-National Faculty

American Teacher: 10th-Grade English Class

The majority of interviewees mentioned that the multi-national faculty was a tremendous asset, exposing students not only to a variety of teaching styles, but also to a variety of cultures, preparing them to build successful careers in many different countries and cultures. As a former Tafari Makonnen School faculty member, I can attest to the tremendous influence of the French-Canadian Jesuit administrators and teachers on the quality of classroom work at Tafari Makonnen. The Jesuits provided me and other faculty members with a model to emulate, and their continuous monitoring and mentoring helped us sharpen our teaching skills.

Encouraging and Fostering Creativity and Innovation

The Jesuit administrators, particularly the "academic dean" Marcel Gareau, encouraged and fostered creativity and innovation in the classroom, which without question strengthened teachers' performance. I learned this in my first semester teaching tenth grade English in 1964. Having been provided with a textbook featuring 18th Century English literature, I found my first few weeks in the classroom frustrating and depressing. I could not figure out how to teach the basics of modern English expression using these culturally-alien, outdated readings, and my students were just as frustrated as I was. I began to lie awake at night worrying that my students might actually walk out of class in the not-too-distant future if I could not come up with a solution.

One night, in the wee hours, a solution I had not considered popped into my mind: I would return the antiquated textbook to the bookstore and write my own textbook, consisting of modern English exercises. Of course, I would have to type a section of my textbook every weekend for the following week's classes, and have copies made in the Director's office. "But will Mr. Gareau take the books back, or will he be offended by my presumptuous behavior as an inexperienced 22-year-old?" I asked myself. The next day, feeling real trepidation, I brought my proposal to the Mr. Gareau, who, to my surprise, took my proposal seriously and graciously agreed to take the assigned textbooks back. Commenting that he was intrigued by my creative solution to the problem of an outdated textbook, he warned me that he would be keeping an cyc on my classes, and if my proposed approach did not succeed, he would expect me to come up with a new solution — pronto. Thank heaven the exercises I developed proved very effective, and I was pleased to present Mr. Gareau with my finished textbook at the end of my first year at TMS.

To take another personal example, my two housemates and fellow TMS teachers, Garber Davidson and Randy Sword, and I brainstormed an initiative to "team-teach" a special ninth grade class consisting of students who had fallen significantly behind the other ninth grade students in the Academic Section and were in serious danger of failing. Our rationale was that the special attention we would provide this class would likely help many if not most of the students catch up and achieve passing grades. I recall that Messrs. Maurice Richer, the director, and Marcel Gareau, the academic "dean," were willing to support the initiative without our having to wage a campaign to overcome their resistance, but now — sixty years later — I must admit that I do not remember how well the experiment went. However, my point is that the Jesuit administrators of Tafari Makonnen School were open to, and highly supportive of, reasonably well-thought-out innovation initiatives in the classroom.

My one-on-one alumni interviews surfaced many less dramatic examples of creativity in the classroom at Tafari Makonnen School. Alumnus Assefa Tsegaye (1951) provided a great example in our interview:

> The quality of education at TMS was incredible. Our education went further than the standard class work. As a case in point, 5A incorporated additional class work such as mental math calculation techniques. . . . Our teacher set up mental math calculation competitions among 5A students. In fact, I and one of my older classmates out-competed the rest of our classmates and reached the "grand finale" competition, which was conducted by the Headmaster of the school . . . who was a very good mental math calculator himself. The competition was held in the auditorium full of students and faculty members. Sadly, I made one error and was not able to win the prize.

You will find other examples of educational innovation in Appendix B.

The Students: Teaching the Teachers

Tafari Makonnen School's student body has always been a key element of the Culture of Excellence — quite the equal of teaching, in my professional opinion. Although Tafari Makonnen School has since its founding been a public institution, its student body has been carefully shaped from its earliest days. Before the Italian occupation, the Emperor heavily relied on provincial governors throughout the country to recommend candidates for admission, and after the occupation, the Jesuit administrators conducted rigorous applicant interviews. The result was a student body consisting of dead-serious scholars whose keen appetite for knowledge and high expectations encouraged teachers to hone their classroom skills. In a very real sense, our students taught us teachers how to take our instruction up a big notch. A fellow history teacher, Garber Davidson, in his memoir "Teaching at Tafari Makonnen School," comments that "What stands out most in my memory of my teaching experience was the sharp interest and attentiveness of my classes." He went on to write:

> I found the students hungry for discussion, and once I had given a brief lecture which took about half of the time allotted for each class, I would open the session for discussion on the topics we were

11th-Grade English Class

currently covering. I was amazed at both the knowledge and insights which the students contributed in these sessions. What was most amazing was their ability to extrapolate from events in the ancient world to their contemporary world. Ethiopia was undergoing the last phase of the monarchy during my tenure, and already cracks in the edifice of the empire were beginning to emerge. The boys were quick to see the parallels between early and later Roman history and the current Ethiopian political situation in particular.

In my experience as a faculty member, I found my students' pride one of their very attractive qualities. They expected to receive — as well as to give — respect. One of my tenth grade English classes the first semester of my first year at TMS taught me a valuable lesson about mutual respect. Returning exam papers one day, I made a sarcastic comment about the generally poor performance of most of the class on the exam. I noticed several shocked expressions, but thought little about it after class. The next morning, when I walked into class no students stood up; they just sat, glowering at me. I could feel my heart thumping. We had been warned in Peace Corps training that Ethiopian students were known to walk out of a poorly taught class. A couple of minutes had passed when the class prefect stood up and said, "Mr. Eadie, we had a meeting before class and decided you had treated us rudely; we expect an apology." I recall feeling threatened initially, but, thank heaven, I realized they were correct, so I said simply "You are right, I was disrespectful, and I apologize." Everyone then stood, we exchanged the usual "good morning," the class sat, and we got to work. I learned a very valuable lesson that day: teachers cannot take their students' respect for granted; they must earn that respect by being respectful in the classroom.

The Role of Ceremony

Also contributing to Tafari Makonnen School's Culture of Excellence has been the use of ceremony to solemnize — and inculcate respect for — the school's educational mission. The morning flag-raising ceremony in front of the iconic administration building, followed by the students' orderly procession to their classrooms was fondly mentioned by many of the alumni I interviewed for this book. Several also favorably cited the end-of-term ceremonies recognizing students' outstanding academic achievement. Several of the alumni I interviewed vividly recall receiving awards for placing first, second, or third in their class from the hands of His Imperial Majesty himself, providing an emphatic affirmation of the importance of learning to Ethiopia's future.

About the End-of-Day Study Hall

Until conducting my one-on-one alumni interviews for this book, I considered the 90-minute study hall that brought the school day to an end a minor feature of the Tafari Makonnen School curriculum. I recall being assigned to monitor my share of study halls as a teacher at Tafari Makonnen, but what I remembered most before conducting my one-on-one interviews was how long and tiring my regular monitoring work made my school day. I certainly did not expect to hear about the required end-of-day study hall from any of my alumni interviewees. How wrong I was! It was, to judge from the great majority of my alumni interviews, a critical feature of Tafari Makonnen School's Culture of Excellence that was mentioned just as often as effective teaching. For example, in my interview with him, alumnus Garedew Atnaf-Seged (1968) described the study hall as "tremendously important," saying that his academic experience at Tafari Makonnen School would have been much weaker without it.

I give full credit to the French-Canadian Jesuits for incorporating the study hall into their design of the post-occupation Tafari Makonnen School, recognizing that the home situations of many if not most students militated against getting their homework accomplished at home, where good lighting and sufficient quiet were in scant supply. Regular, often challenging homework assignments helped to make academic excellence a hallmark of Tafari Makonnen School, hence making the daily study hall an important feature of the Culture of Excellence.

Order and Discipline

One day in the second semester of my second year as a Tafari Makonnen faculty member I was standing outside of the office of Mr. Gerard Gagnon, the Jesuit Assistant Director in charge of student discipline at that time, waiting for our scheduled conference, when I heard several slaps and crying. When the door opened, Mr. Gagnon ushered out a boy in tears. Shocked and upset, I made very clear what I thought about corporal punishment — initially by my expression, not words. By way of explanation, he said something along the lines of "We must adapt to the culture if we want to maintain order." I recall responding in a shaky voice that nothing, absolutely nothing could justify corporal punishment in an educational institution.

I believed, and continue to believe, that a really capable teacher does not need to employ physical violence to maintain order in his or her classes.

The reader can imagine my surprise when the great majority of alumni in my one-on-one interviews for this book cited discipline and order as critical positive features of their Tafari Makonnen experience. Only one alumnus, as I recall, testified that the corporal punishment employed at Tafari Makonnen School was excessive. I am willing to admit that my stance against corporal punishment might have, under the circumstances, been naïve and wrong-headed, if, indeed, it was culturally necessary to preserve order. And experience as a TMS faculty member taught me that order in the classroom was essential to effective teaching and learning.

Holistic Education at Tafari Makonnen School

A Wide Array of Extracurricular Opportunities

Fr. Festo Mkenda, in *A Splash of Diamond*, observes that while the Jesuits were developing the academic building blocks of the post-Italian occupation Tafari Makonnen School, "changes were being introduced to make the school a well-rounded Jesuit institution for the formation of the whole person, focusing on physical fitness, personal discipline, and team spirit." Virtually every alumnus I interviewed for this book testified that the resulting rich array of "extracurricular" opportunities, including sports such as football, volleyball, track and field, and a wide variety of clubs, engaged students in current events, debating, theater, and music, making their Tafari Makonnen experience more satisfying and meaningful.

These extracurricular activities were for the most part carefully planned and managed to ensure that students would have a powerful learning experience, as alumnus Temesgen Petros (1966) indicates in his description of the Radio Club in his book *The Story of My Life*:

> TMS had a radio station run under the supervision of Father Payeur, our science teacher, who created the radio broadcasting services within the school campus. The club had 2 tape recorders, 1 record player, 1 amplifier, 2 loud speakers, 2 microphones and several cassette tapes recorded with a variety of contemporary musical songs. The station used to broadcast daily news and music within the school

campus during break hours. I was a member of the club and elected to serve as the secretary along with my classmate, Ato Petros Aklilu, who served as the president of the club. With our joint efforts, our broadcasting services were phenomenal and . . .appreciated by Father Payeur and all our audience. In the same year, the club was invited and we visited the Ethiopian radio station in Addis Ababa.

Current Affairs Club

The Jesuit administrators assigned faculty members to serve as advisers for the various clubs, not only helping to ensure their success but also providing important opportunities for teachers and students to interact and get to know each other better. I can testify from experience that the Jesuits expected faculty members to take the advisory role seriously. When I was asked to serve as adviser to the Current Affairs Club and to be the American Field Service faculty representative on campus, Mr. Gareau provided me with a detailed orientation on my advisory responsibilities, asked me to prepare a workplan for each assignment, which he reviewed and discussed with me, and he and I met to review progress at least once a month. By the way, on the bookcase in my study at home is a photograph of me with a much younger version of Bisrat Aklilu, TMSAA President and CEO, along with other Tafari Makonnen students selected for the American Field Service program.

The Tafari Makonnen School Boy Scouts: Character Building Par Excellence

The Boy Scouts program at Tafari Makonnen School deserves special attention in light of its tremendous impact on participants, including the focus on character building, and the inspired leadership of its faculty adviser, the much-loved Paul Beaudry, who had a profound personal impact on many Scouts. According to Abebe Abraham Joteh (1968), the Scouting program was "life changing for me." Abebe vividly recalls the song he learned as a Scout to sing at the end of every day: "Silently, each Scout should ask, Have I done my daily task? Have I kept my honor bright? Can I guiltless sleep tonight?" See Appendix C for Abebe's detailed account of his Scouting experience.

Boy Scouts at Lake Langano with Mr. Gareau

Dr. Moges Gebremariam (1965) writes in a post at the blog "Entwined Lives" that he was "immersed in the Boy Scouts at TMS":

> I prided myself on earning and collecting merit badges. I enjoyed the campfires, hikes, trips to nearby places like Tinsis, Washa-Mickael and Akaki's AZ Pool . . . as well as faraway places like Awssa, Langano, Chercher, and Harar. Out Scout master Father Beaudry's devotion to us was unparalleled. Every opportunity he got, in groups large and small, or individually, he never tired of counseling us. He convinced me to become a doctor. "Healing the sick, caring for the poor is a noble profession pioneered by St. Luke and Christ himself," he used to repeat to me. I, therefore, abandoned my favorite subject, geography, and Father Turenne, my geography teacher, to join the Faculty of Science at Haile Selassie I University.

The Scouting program enriched the Tafari Makonnen School experience of faculty advisers as well as students. Garber Davidson vividly recalls participating in the Scout holiday camps:

> During the summers I had volunteered to be a scout master, and to work with one of the Jesuit instructors, a favorite teacher and colleague who later came to the U.S. to participate in the Christening of my oldest son. His name was Paul Beaudry. He had been active with the scout troops for many years. We would take the troops out of the city to camp at the lakes south of Addis, and when we arrived at the campsite, the first order of business was for the Jesuits to set up a rather full bar. It was a refreshing change from my own scout experience, which emphasized all of the more mundane tasks such as setting up tents, digging latrines, etc. At the campfires in the evenings, I recall the marvelous music that elicited a rapturous kind of dancing by the boys. Spontaneously the boys would join in the rhythmic dances of Ethiopia, and this light show of virtuosity would continue until the wee hours of the night. This was an opportunity to see the spirit of Ethiopia's young people — regardless of their economic status, their

tribal heritage or their family backgrounds — all equally participating with great enthusiasm in this natural celebration of both their own individual development and their identity with their fellow Ethiopian students. It was always a great thrill to watch this unfold.

Like Garber Davidson, I fondly recall the time I spent at the Boy Scout holiday camp at Lake Langano, especially sitting with Paul Beaudry and other faculty members outside his tent as the sun sank in the west, enjoying cocktails, cigars, and wide-ranging discussion, and the nightly singing and dancing around the campfire. Not a Boy Scout growing up in the United States, I was surprised and pleased to be invited to join the camp as "honorary camp historian," a title Paul invented for my special case, so far as I know. It was not an onerous role; at least, I do not recall producing any historical essays documenting the camp experience. Observing Paul closely during our couple of weeks together at Langano, I better understood what a unique figure he had become in the Tafari Makonnen "family," at once a revered authority figure dispensing advice and modeling what being a man of character means, while also thoroughly enjoying his casual time with the Scouts he so loved.

Other Teacher-Student Interaction Outside the Classroom

Messrs. Richer and Gareau both encouraged me and my faculty colleagues to interact casually with our students outside the classroom as a means to enrich and strengthen the teacher-student bond — with a strong caveat. It was very simple: first thoroughly master your primary role: teaching, and make sure you are in full command in the classroom, leading, not following, your students. I remember well Mr. Gareau reminding me that education was a serious business in Ethiopia; my students' future heavily depended on their academic success, and my preeminent job was to prepare them to succeed academically. Then, having firmly established myself in the classroom, I could feel free to cultivate a more informal relationship with my students. Many of my faculty colleagues and I embraced this extracurricular role with enthusiasm, consequently infusing our Tafari Makonnen experience with deeper emotional satisfaction.

One tradition my housemates and I established the second semester of our first teaching year was to invite our classes to join us on weekends at our home across from Empress Menen School for refreshments, occasional movies, and open discussion covering a wide range of topics. I recall my tenth-grade students loving the film "Years of Lightning, Day of Drums," about John F. Kennedy's presidency and assassination in November 1963, feeling tremendous pride at Emperor Haile Selassie's warm welcome as President and Mrs. Kennedy's honored guest at the White House and seeing the Emperor walk with other world leaders down Pennsylvania Avenue in President Kennedy's funeral procession to Arlington National Cemetery. My housemates and I responded candidly to any questions our students asked during these "at-homes," many on sensitive issues such as racism in the US, I recall many of the students at one of our Saturday get-togethers looking quite surprised to learn that I — the son of a small town bakery owner — was able to attend the University of Illinois despite my modest background. By the way, one of my co-authors of this book, Abebe Abraham Joteh, appears in a photo I took at home on one of those Saturday open houses.

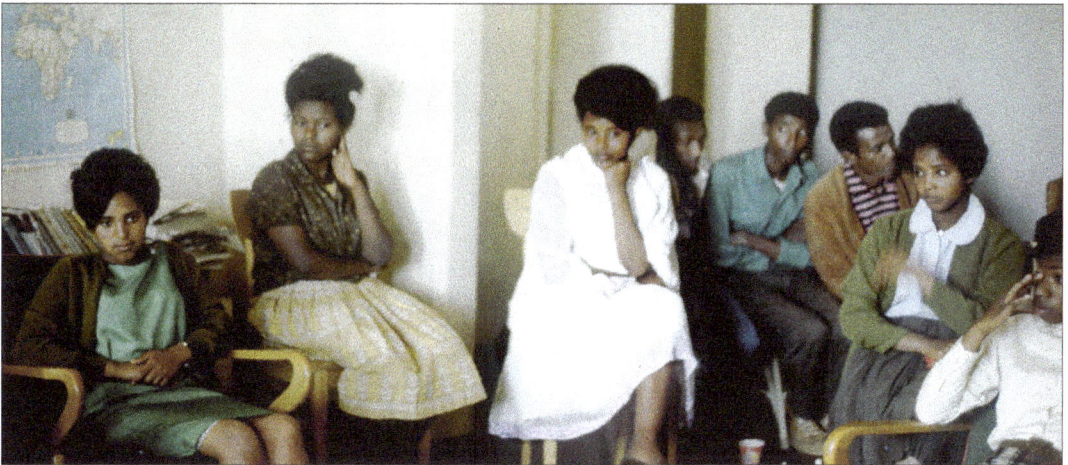

Saturday at Home

Among my fondest memories of casual interactions with my students are the "field" trips with my classes to notable places in Addis Ababa, such as the Commercial Bank of Ethiopia and Africa Hall, where I arranged for senior executives from these institutions to speak and answer student questions. I forget when we invented and began to play an enjoyable game on our long walks around Addis: our students competing to identify and correct English grammar and spelling mistakes on signs we passed on our way to and from notable locations. Never was the process of strengthening their command of English more pleasant for my students — and also for me.

Field Trip to Africa Hall

Coda: A Labor of Love

It is both a privilege and an honor to be invited to serve as one of the co-authors of this book about a distinguished educational institution that has made so many lives fuller and more satisfying than they might otherwise have been and that has through its illustrious alumni played a key role in Ethiopia's development. At a more personal and emotional level, helping to create this book has also been a true labor of love, partly because I am in a sense an alumnus of Tafari Makonnen School, having over the course of my three years as a TMS faculty member mastered the fine art of teaching, with the help of hundreds of bright, hard-working students whose high expectations were a tremendous motivator. My emotional commitment to this book also has much to do with how I happened to be at Tafari Makonnen School in the first place and how — almost sixty years after returning to the United States from Ethiopia — I became engaged with Bisrat Aklilu and the Tafari Makonnen School Alumni Association.

It is serendipity that led me to Addis Ababa, Ethiopia and Tafari Makonnen School. In December of 1963, I — a 21-year-old senior at the University of Illinois at Champaign-Urbana — was strolling through the Illini Student Union. I was, I recall, thinking about my first semester of law school that would begin that coming September. I passed a table where two young ladies were sitting. On the wall behind the table was a poster showing an earnest-looking young man driving a Land Rover on a dirt road with acacia trees in the distance and, at the top, "Join the Peace Corps and See the World."

I walked past the table fifteen feet or so and stopped. I vividly recall thinking "Doug, why in heaven's name are you headed for three years of law school. You haven't traveled farther than Chicago 100 miles north; you haven't had any adventures; you haven't done anything really significant: only studying and earning a string of A's." So I turned around, walked back to that table, and asked one of the young ladies if the Peace Corps needed teachers. "Thousands," she said, and invited me to return to the Student Union that evening to take a Peace Corps aptitude test. I did, and in three weeks or so I received a letter from Peace Corps headquarters in Washington, DC, informing me that I had been "pre-selected" for the Peace Corps and was guaranteed an assignment, and asking me what country I wanted to serve in. After a long conversation with my housemate over dinner that evening, I sent my response: "anywhere in Africa."

In early January 1964, a letter from Peace Corps headquarters arrived, informing me that I was to report to the third Peace Corps Ethiopia Teacher Training Program at the University of California at Los Angeles early that June of 1964. Reading the letter, I was reminded of a dramatic scene I had witnessed with friends from the U of I on November 25, 1963. We had driven all night from Champaign-Urbana to Washington, DC, to pay homage to our murdered hero, President John F. Kennedy, who founded the Peace Corps. Standing on the street that sad day of President Kennedy's funeral, as the funeral procession made its way to Arlington Cemetery, for the first time I saw in person His Imperial Majesty Haile Selassie I of Ethiopia, walking in the procession with other world leaders. I recall being struck by his regal bearing; he looked every inch an emperor.

That September I arrived in Addis Ababa with three hundred-some "Ethi IIIs," as we were known, and soon learned I was assigned to Tafari Makonnen School, a short walk from the Empress Menen School dormitory where we were temporarily housed. Before the first day of class, two other Peace Corps Volunteers assigned to TMS, Garber Davidson and Randy Sword, and I rented a house directly across the street from Empress Menen's gate. My life had changed so dramatically in such a short time that I think I was still in a kind of daze. Quite a journey for a man of only 22 who had grown up in a small Illinois farm town, who had never traveled farther than the 150-mile trip to Chicago, and whose first time in an airplane was the flight to Los Angeles for Peace Corps training. Not planned, not even imagined! A classic case of serendipity in action.

Foreign Dignitaries in the President's Funeral Procession

Some of the many foreign dignitaries marching behind the coffin of the late President John F. Kennedy as the funeral procession left the White House today. In the front row (from left) are: PRESIDENT HEINRICH LUBKE of West Germany, PRESIDENT CHARLES DE GAULLE of France, QUEEN FREDERIKA of Greece, KING BAUDOUIN of Belgium, EMPEROR HAILE SELASSIE of Ethiopia and PRESIDENT DIOSDADO MACAPAGAL of the Philippines.

Associated Press Wirephoto

Emperor Haile Selassie in JFK Funeral Procession, November 25, 1963

As it turned out, I loved every minute teaching at Tafari Makonnen School for three years, and I was for several months after returning to the US for graduate school in 1967 quite "homesick" for the school and Addis Ababa generally. Back "home" in my own country, I felt like a bit of a misfit after my happy years at Tafari Makonnen. Of course, as the years passed, the homesickness for Ethiopia eased, and my time at Tafari Makonnen School became a fond memory. But a little over a decade into the twenty-first century, Tafari Makonnen came back into my life in a major way. I reunited with one of my most outstanding Tafari Makonnen students at the fiftieth reunion of the Peace Corps, Abebe Abraham Joteh, in 2011, and I returned to Ethiopia a year later to visit a Tafari Makonnen School alumnus who had lived with me and my housemates for two years, Tesfagiorgis Wondimagegnehu, who had been imprisoned under the Derg.

Not long after my reunion with Tesfagiorgis, I began to write about my teaching experience at Tafari Makonnen School in a blog I created, "Entwined Lives," and reunited with another outstanding former student, Bisrat Aklilu, who invited me to address a General Assembly of what was then known as the Tafari Makonnen School Alumni Association of North America, And when in early 2024 I decided to retire at last and was investigating volunteer opportunities, the perfect one came along at Bisrat's invitation: contributing to this book. A full circle, to be sure!

Appendix A
Tesfagiorgis' Story

I had grown very close to Tesfagiorgis during the 2 ½ years he had lived with me and my Peace Corps housemates while he studied, and we taught at Tafari Makonnen School. By the time I headed back to the States for graduate school in June 1967, Tesfagiorgis had become, I realize looking back, very much my kid brother. My last few weeks in Ethiopia the summer of 1967 were so busy I did not really think much about the impact my leaving might have on Tesfagiorgis and the other Tafari Makonnen student living with us then, Tariku Belay. There were final examination papers to mark, graduate school arrangements to make, travel plans to finalize, packing to do — so much in so little time. Anyway, Tesfagiorgis and Tariku, soon to graduate from Ethiopia's finest secondary school, were seemingly on their way to a promising future. I need not worry, I thought; they were well launched.

The years passed quickly; life went on as it is wont to do. Tesfagiorgis and I corresponded now and then as he completed his undergraduate work at what was then Haile Selassie I University and began his career in public administration at the Ethiopian government's Central Personnel Agency. In the meantime, I completed my graduate work, launched a career in nonprofit management, and eventually married and started a family. Sometime in 1974, after Emperor Haile Selassie's overthrow by the Derg, Tesfagiorgis and I fell out of touch. As I followed events in Ethiopia in the *New York Times* in the mid to late 1970s, I realized that attempting to contact Tesfagiorgis might actually put his life in danger. I stopped writing, and no more letters from Tesfagiorgis arrived. Thus did our physical separation become a complete break. By the time the new century arrived, I assumed Tesfagiorgis and Tariku had very likely died under the brutal dictator Mengistu Haile Mariam. In 2008, thank heaven, my assumption proved erroneous.

Tariku tracked me down in November 2008, and we reunited in Minneapolis, Minnesota, where he was teaching in a public high school, a little over a year later. It turned out that he had been in prison under the Derg, had escaped and lived as a refugee in the Sudan before coming to the States. The night before I was to leave for Minneapolis for our reunion, Tariku called to tell me exciting news. He had discovered that Tesfagiorgis was alive and well, retired and living with his wife in Addis Ababa. His daughter was studying in the States, in Boston. He gave me Tesfagiorgis' telephone number, which I called right after we hung up. Tesfagiorgis was home and answered the phone. We were both soon in tears. "This is a miracle," he said. I wholeheartedly agreed.

I began to think seriously about returning to Ethiopia after my forty-four-year absence the fall of 2011 while attending the 50th anniversary celebration of the Peace Corps in Washington, where I reunited with a former Tafari Makonnen student, Abebe Abraham Joteh, and with former Addis Ababa housemates and fellow TMS teachers Garber Davidson, David Karro, and Mike Altman. Meanwhile, Tesfagiorgis and I had been carrying on a robust email correspondence, and the more I learned about his life after my departure back in 1967, the more miraculous our discovering each other seemed. My wife, Barbara, and my kids, Jenny and Will, strongly encouraged me to make the return trip, pointing out that I was not getting any younger and might someday terribly regret missing this wonderful opportunity.

Now let me tell you some of what I learned about Tesfagiorgis' experience under the Derg as we sat across from each other in my hotel room in Addis Ababa in May 2012, filming the video clip, and I think you will agree that our reuniting is, indeed, a miracle.

I do not recall that Tesfagiorgis and I spent much time chatting about Ethiopian politics while he was living with me and my Peace Corps housemates, but his political awakening was not long in coming after his graduation from Tafari Makonnen and enrollment in Haile Selassie I University. Those were heady and hopeful times, as students throughout Ethiopia, sensing that the old feudal order that Emperor Haile Selassie represented was near death, saw a wonderful opportunity to play a leading role in creating a new, presumably more democratic, Ethiopia. Tesfagiorgis certainly jumped in with both feet, for example, participating in demonstrations against the Ian Smith regime in Southern Rhodesia and the government's banning of the Ethiopian University Students Union and passing out leaflets protesting the murder of a student movement leader. Indeed, Tesfagiorgis was one of a small number of fourth year students at the University suspended for a full year because of their refusal to stop boycotting classes until imprisoned student leaders were released.

The "dark days" that Tesfagiorgis so fervently hoped to forget began not long after the Derg overthrew the tottering regime of Emperor Haile Selassie in 1974. As the revolt against the Emperor was gaining momentum, Tesfagiorgis received his bachelor's degree from the University and began his public administration career at the government's Central Personnel Agency. He continued to be politically active, joining one of the new political parties that emerged in these tumultuous times: the Ethiopian Peoples' Revolutionary Party (EPRP), which eventually became passionately and violently opposed to the Derg. He also assumed leadership roles in the new political structure established by the Derg, being elected chairman of one of the 283 local urban dwellers associations known as "kebeles," and also of the political discussion forum that had been created in the Central Personnel Agency. When the Derg declared all-out war on EPRP, empowering kebeles to arrest, torture, and execute Ethiopians suspected of being EPRP supporters, Tesfagiorgis found himself leading an extremely stressful and highly dangerous double life that eventually resulted in his imprisonment and near-execution.

One of the stories that Tesfagiorgis told as we shot the video clip in my hotel room had to do with an invitation to his kebele from a neighboring kebele to participate in the interrogation of some suspected EPRP supporters. Because Tesfagiorgis's kebele was suspected of disloyalty, the invitation to participate could not safely be refused, so he and his close friend and reliable kebele colleague, Gebrehiwot Asfaw, along with some other kebele colleagues, went to the neighboring kebele late one evening. What Tesfagiorgis witnessed that evening left him shaken and fearful, knowing that he could all too easily become a victim himself. Watching two or three of the suspects being suspended between two tables and having the soles of their bare feet viciously beaten with sticks and cables was horrifying enough. But he could not have imagined what would happen next. One young prisoner from Tesfagiorgis's kebele was told to take off his jacket and shirt and lie down on a table, to which his hands and feet were tied. One of the guards then put gasoline-soaked papers on the young man's bare chest and set them afire. Crying and begging for mercy, the young man soon lost consciousness, was untied and thrown on the floor. As Tesfagiorgis observed, "I started to seriously think about myself and knew something worse was hovering over my head."

Things grew ever more dangerous and nerve wracking for Tesfagiorgis, who as chairman of his kebele was forced to participate in door-to-door searches for EPRP supporters. "Arrests and killings were widespread," according to Tesfagiorgis, "and survival was a daily worry of the young and their parents and relatives. Seeing bodies of people killed and thrown in the streets became more and more common." Tesfagiorgis' exhausting and frightening double life came to an end when he was arrested early in 1978. After being interrogated and forced to make a videoed public confession on a stage at the Central Personnel Agency, Tesfagiorgis served two years in prison. One of his most horrifying memories from his two years in prison was when at 4:00 a.m. one day, twelve of his fellow inmates, including two newly made friends, were taken — hands tied — out of the cell and executed, their bodies thrown in the street and left there for a half day for the public to see. By the way, Tesfagiorgis later found out from a former official now imprisoned with him that "whenever he saw me, I reminded him of a miracle, and the miracle was my survival. He told me that I survived that bloody night by a single vote in my favor. I could have been the 13th person to be executed. That made things fresh in my mind and made me sleepless again for some days. I never knew who voted for and against my life."

Tesfagiorgis' dark days eventually came to an end. He suffered terribly, but he is keenly aware how fortunate he was to have survived, when thousands did not. He is grateful to have been able to return to the Central Personnel Agency (which became the Civil Service Commission), where he was blessed to resume the life of achievement that Tafari Makonnen School had prepared him to lead, including service as the Chief Position Classification Analyst and Head of the Planning, Policy Analysis and Review Department. After his retirement from government service, Tesfagiorgis worked as Assistant to the Manager, Human Resources and Administration Department, at the Awash International Bank and at KAKI PLC a large private company engaged in exporting agricultural commodities.

Appendix B
More on Encouraging Creative Experiments

I conducted a rather radical educational experiment the first semester of my second year as a Tafari Makonnen teacher that bore fruit. I had not run it by Mr. Gareau because it was implemented on the spot, with absolutely no forethought, much less advance planning, and certainly without Mr. Gareau's prior seal of approval. The Tafari Makonnen School Director, Mr. Maurice Richer, had asked me to teach an 11th grade girls' English class in the Commercial Section, which I only very reluctantly agreed to do because of my full teaching load and my sneaking suspicion that the Commercial Section might not uphold the school's high academic standards. My first month of class was, to say the least, dispiriting. My students, although clearly quite bright, were apparently unmotivated and definitely underachieving. Homework assignments were often late and generally sloppily done, and quiz results on the whole miserable.

One day, I reacted to another set of poorly done homework assignments by announcing to the class that I worked too hard to put up with their lethargic behavior, so I was leaving the class in the hands of the prefect and was not sure I would ever return. Without another word, I walked across campus to the teachers' room on the second floor of the administration building and was marking copybooks when fifteen minutes or so after my abrupt exit, I heard shuffling on the stairs and found the whole class lined up. They had met, the prefect informed me, and had decided to begin working much harder if I would return to class. I did, we finished the period, and, true to their word, my eleventh graders became an exemplary class.

Reflecting on the incident years later, while co-authoring this book, I have concluded that my Jesuit superiors had expected me to do something dramatic in response to my eleventh graders' complacent underachievement. I cannot be sure, but they had to be aware of my dramatic exit from class that day, and not one of the top three Jesuit administrators, Messrs. Richer, Gagnon, and Gareau, asked me for an explanation. I can only conclude that their commitment to innovation was rock-solid, even when that innovation was, like mine, well outside the norm, By the way, Fr. Festo Mkenda, SJ, author of *A Splash of Diamond*, laughingly agreed with my conclusion when I shared this story with him a few months ago.

On a lighter note, my colleague and housemate, Randy Sword, who taught ninth grade biology, set a high standard for audacious innovation in the classroom at Tafari Makonnen School, by adding a very candid sex education module to his biology curriculum — and, by the way, as my readers can imagine, earned tremendous popularity as a consequence. My ninth-grade ancient history class followed Randy's biology class, and I will never forget walking into class one day after Randy's biology session and finding the blackboard's folding leaves closed. My mind was on the Code of Hammurabi, so I barely noticed the tittering going on as I unpacked my briefcase at the front of the room and turned to open the backboard. Confronted by large, brightly colored chalk drawings vividly illustrating the "facts of life," I stood there dumbstruck while my students screamed with laughter. When I asked Randy about the incident in a Zoom call recently, over sixty years after his perpetrating the foul deed, he testified that he never received the least hint of a reprimand from any Jesuit administrator — not that he could recall, anyway. I recall being both greatly amused by the incident and somewhat envious of Randy's easily won popularity. Ancient history could not compete!

Appendix C
Abebe Abraham Joteh Reflects on His Scouting Experience

Author's Note: I am pleased that Abebe Abraham Joteh, an outstanding former student of mine at TMS, contributed this first-person memoir to Chapter One.

The impact of our time at Tafari Makonnen School (TMS) becomes increasingly meaningful as we reflect on it. For many of us, those years were profoundly formative, shaping not only our academic skills but also instilling the leadership qualities that have guided us throughout our lives. Personal stories from our time at TMS are enduring testaments to the school's unique environment and its influence. Whether through involvement in extracurricular activities or leadership roles within student organizations, we learned the value of responsibility, resilience, and collaboration.

Each day, we should reflect and ask ourselves if we have fulfilled our duties.

While at TMS, the concept of Adera deeply inspired me, encouraging me to walk a straight path. However, it was the Boy Scouts program under Father Paul Beaudry that provided the practical framework to put these values into action. We were each given a small notebook, where we were encouraged to document our daily charitable deeds, transforming abstract ideals into tangible actions. This practice became a guide for us — helping us translate the principles we learned into daily habits.

Silently, each scout was prompted to ask: *Have I completed my daily task? Have I kept my honor bright? Can I rest tonight with a clear conscience?*

These words, coupled with the vision of our founders and the spirit of Adera, offered solace and guidance amid the complexities of daily life. They served as a beacon, encouraging us to work diligently toward goals that not only benefit ourselves but also contribute to the well-being of our families, our organizations, and our communities. This framework shaped our understanding of leadership, teaching us that true success is helping others with dedication on a sustained basis.

One vivid memory from my time at TMS is a summer tour to Bahirdar, where I was assigned the duty to organize the coordination for a day. Faced with resistance from two peers, I had to make challenging decisions to maintain order and enhance the success of the tour. This experience became a defining moment in my leadership journey — teaching me the importance of standing firm, making tough calls, and leading with integrity. These lessons, learned beyond the classroom, proved as valuable as any academic achievement.

During one of our tours to historical sites, I was tasked with planning and assigning teams for the day's meals. I meticulously paired individuals, assigning two people per task to cover meal planning and preparation. Most accepted their roles willingly and began their tasks, but two men refused to cooperate. Attempting to assert their dominance, they questioned my authority, confident that their larger size and alliance would intimidate me. Instead of confronting them directly, I calmly reassigned their tasks to others and informed the dissenters that they would not receive dinner that evening because of their refusal. This decision angered them further and they resorted to threats to make me back down. However, I held my ground, understanding that compromising would undermine my leadership.

Gezmu Eshete, a Senior Rover Scout supervising the trip, soon learned of the situation. Known for his physical presence as well as his intellect and leadership qualities, he swiftly approached the duo and with a no-nonsense attitude, he warned the two men that their behavior would not be tolerated and that they would face grave consequences if they continued their defiance. His commanding presence and unwavering resolve left no room for argument. Realizing they were outmatched, the two men backed down and ultimately went without dinner — a fitting consequence for their behavior.

This experience taught me a crucial lesson: effective leadership often requires making tough decisions and remaining steadfast, even in the face of intimidation. Bravery is not about physical strength; it is about having the conviction to stand by the right decision and move forward with confidence.

Chapter Two
Lives of Achievement:
Fifty Profiles

የተፈሪ:መኮንን፥ትምሀርት:ቤት።
Tafari Makonnen School

100 ፻ው

1925–2025

Alem W. Mathias, Contributor
TMS Class of 1970
Vice President, Tafari Makonnen School
Alumni Association (TMSAA)

Lives of Achievement: Fifty Profiles

It is an honor and a privilege to contribute to the Tafari Makonnen School (TMS) centennial publication. This book brings together authors and accomplished professionals from across disciplines, unified by their shared connection to this historic institution. TMS is more than a school; it is a beacon of excellence that has shaped the lives of countless alumni, including three of this book's contributors: Dr. Bisrat Aklilu, Abebe Abraham Joteh and myself. The project, which has been generously spearheaded by Doug Eadie — a former TMS teacher and a distinguished author — captures the essence of TMS's legacy. Doug's passion for teaching and his admiration for TMS and its students are genuinely reflected in this book in a way that warms the heart. A sought-after speaker, board and CEO adviser and management coach, Doug has a strong connection to TMS, and his heartfelt commitment to the school we love is clearly visible throughout this book.

My task was to highlight and summarize the remarkable accomplishments of fifty extraordinary alumni — no easy task given TMS has graduated generations of leaders and pioneers. Even in narrowing the biographies to willing TMSAA members, their stories are incredibly rich, their accomplishments numerous, and yet our space here is limited. Still, even in brief, the contributions and achievements of my peers reflect great individual success, but also — and importantly — the collective spirit of TMS, which continues to inspire greatness across generations.

Historical Context

Founded with a vision of fostering academic excellence and moral character, TMS stands as a testament to the power of education. Its foundation was laid by His Royal Highness Crown Prince Ras Tafari Makonnen, who was passionately committed to the advancement of his country and its people. Through its rigorous curriculum, disciplined environment, and emphasis on personal integrity, TMS has cultivated leaders across diverse fields. More than an academic center, this institution has been a vessel where students are molded into future nation-builders and changemakers.

Reading the biographies of my fellow alumni was an emotional journey down memory lane. In their diverse and remarkable achievements, I saw reflections of my own experiences. Some alumni have served or are serving Ethiopia through roles in the private sector, government, and international agencies, while others have made their mark elsewhere outside of Ethiopia and even on a global scale. Each, "according to his or her lot," has created meaningful and lasting impacts. Delving into their stories — both at TMS and throughout their careers — brought my own journey into sharper perspective, underscoring the shared legacy of excellence and service that binds us all.

Early Life and Education

My journey began in Ethiopia in the 1950s as the eldest of ten siblings. Growing up, I was shaped by the unwavering support of my parents and extended family, who instilled in me values of hard work, faith, and resilience. These foundational principles set the course for the path forward. My early education began at a traditional priest school, where discipline and spirituality were paramount, and continued at Nativity Girls School where I thrived both academically and socially. As a young girl, I was inspired by my experience assisting my father, a talented goldsmith, in his jewelry shop where I learned the importance of diligence, responsibility and customer service.

TMS Years

Admission to Tafari Makonnen School marked a pivotal moment in my life. TMS provided a world-class education and opened doors to explore my full potential. It emphasized holistic development, blending academics with extracurricular activities that shaped our lives and leadership skills. The numerous clubs that provided structured ways to learn about giving back to our community, supporting one another, and gaining the confidence needed to face the world beyond the classroom were transformative. These clubs, each guided by an advisor or a teacher, instilled in us a sense of duty and fellowship, teaching us that while individual success was important, collective growth and responsibility toward each other were just as vital.

From participating in the school's on-campus radio station and student-run bank to joining clubs like choir and charity, I discovered the value of teamwork and community engagement, which have been cornerstones of TMS. As members of the charity club, my peers and I, with full support from the Assistant Director, Mr. Gagnon, were allowed to open a small tea shop in the recreation area. We each contributed seed money to purchase tea and breakfast products that we regularly sold to students in the early morning hours and during school breaks. We then used the proceeds to support programs for the underprivileged. Through TMS's Literacy Outreach Program, under Mr. Payeur's supervision, we helped women become more literate in nearby communities. Little did we realize at the time that we were already experiencing the purpose and privilege of committing ourselves to service — a value that would later become the cornerstone of our future home, the United States.

Another remarkable aspect of our education was the exposure we had to instructors from diverse cultures and backgrounds. In addition to the finest Ethiopian educators, we also had inspiring teachers from the US, India, Canada, Ireland, Armenia and France, which enriched our learning experiences and broadened our perspectives. They helped us see beyond our immediate surroundings. We learned about the world through the eyes and teachings of those who brought different viewpoints, experiences, and teaching styles into the classroom. We interacted with them in an atmosphere of mutual respect, fostering relationships that transcended the traditional teacher-student dynamic. They were our mentors and their belief in us and their commitment to our success motivated us to work harder, aim higher, and push beyond our perceived limitations.

It was with the help of our teachers and administrators that TMS's student council was established. Looking back, I remember what a defining moment our 1967 election was for all of us. The process, in introspect, mirrored what we considered should be the real-world political landscape, especially in our country where the government had yet to implement elections for its own president. We engaged in every aspect of a democratic process — nominations, campaigns, debates, and elections — and each step was filled with excitement, anticipation, and sometimes even the negativities that come with competition. At the end, we understood that regardless of the outcome, we were all working toward the same goal: improving our school community and setting a strong example of civility for the younger generation. Inspired by that experience, six years later I ran for election for my college student council and served as treasurer for two years.

At TMS we were encouraged to dream big, to strive for excellence, and to embrace challenges with confidence. Our teachers were unwavering in their expectations, yet supportive in their approach. They didn't allow us to settle for mediocrity, and in return, we strived to make them proud, knowing that our achievements reflected not only on us but on the teachers and parents who had invested in us. That sense of pride and responsibility shaped us into adults who carried those values into our careers, families, and communities.

Beyond the invaluable personal and educational growth, TMS also became the backdrop to one of the greatest blessings of my life — meeting my wonderful future husband, Hilletework Mathias. He, too, was an alumnus of TMS who had graduated before me, and as fate would have it, he returned to the school under the National Service Program to teach in the technical section for one year. It was during this time that our paths crossed, later leading to marriage in 1978 in the US. Together, we have raised two incredible daughters and are now blessed with two precious grandchildren, bringing immense joy to our lives. I am forever indebted to him for all his support and encouragement and for making me a better person.

Post-TMS Education

The political instability in Ethiopia during the early 1970s disrupted my studies at the Haile Selassie I University, prompting me to move to the United States. Despite the challenges of being far from home, compounded by the sudden loss of my father, I remained steadfast in my pursuit of education with the hope of returning to Ethiopia right after graduation. I enrolled in a business administration program, where I excelled academically, graduating magna cum laude in 1975. Unfortunately, I was unable to return home.

In building a life for myself in the United States, however, I have seen the profound goodness of humanity reflected by its selfless citizens in several ways. Their strong work ethics, their acts of kindness, their generous donations of time and resources to communities in need continue to be a great inspiration to many.

Pursuing my first professional job was daunting, but someone saw my potential and guided me to a position with CSX Corporation, a Fortune 500 railroad company. TMS's vocational training in commerce and shorthand proved invaluable, enabling me to secure a highly competitive position at a crucial time. After being hired on a temporary basis in 1976, I worked hard to prove myself, earning a permanent position and a sponsored resident visa that allowed me to embark on a rewarding and decades-long growth journey at CSX. I progressed from a customer service representative to leadership roles, including Manager of Government Relations and Director of Political Affairs. My work included overseeing federal and state political action committees (PACs), leading compliance research, and managing high-profile events and programs.

CSX invested in my professional development, enabling me to expand my horizon in legislative processes, campaign laws, and administration. My contributions earned recognition, including the prestigious Corporate Masters Award and a notable mention in President Reagan's "War on Waste" initiative.

Beyond building my corporate career, I was able to successfully balance entrepreneurship guided by ambition and a passion for creating opportunities.

I give thanks for the sacrifices of my family, the dedication of my teachers, the inspiration of my friends, and the invaluable support of my bosses, mentors and the community. Together, they have left an indelible mark on my life, shaping me into someone who strives to live — like so many of my fellow TMS alumni — with gratitude, humility, and a commitment to paying forward the kindness I have been so fortunate to receive.

Reflections on TMS Alumni

The fifty alumni profiled in this book are from all sections of Ethiopia and a testament to the transformative power of TMS. While their countless achievements have been significantly summarized in the following pages, the highlights alone demonstrate the incredible impact they have delivered across education, economics, medicine, finance and the arts. They have excelled as professors, military leaders, physicians, engineers, entrepreneurs, lawyers, consultants, and CEOs leaving a lasting impression on their communities and beyond. Each alumnus's story is a reflection of TMS's enduring legacy embodying the values of excellence, integrity, and service that the school stands for. It is a distinct privilege to present their "Lives of Achievement."

Profiles of TMS Graduates

Compiled by Alem W. Mathias

Aklilu Habte, PhD
TMS Class of 1950

Dr. Aklilu Habte was born in September 1929 in Addis Ababa, Ethiopia. He combines thirty-six years (1958-1994) of academic, managerial, national and international civil service experience, and over 23 years of selective consultancy services, Civil Society Organizations and Diaspora Religious Community volunteer activities. Distinguished fellow of the Academy for Educational Development, Dr. Aklilu is author of several articles, monographs and reports on education and development including his latest book on higher education in Ethiopia with emphasis on the history of Haile Selassie I University.

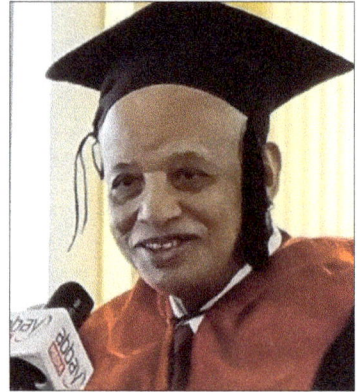

Education

- Bachelor's Degree with distinction from the University College of Addis Ababa later to become Haile Selassie I University; (1954)
- Bachelor of Education, University of Manitoba, Canada (1955)
- Master of Education and Doctorate from Ohio State University (1956 and 1958) Hon. D.H.L. from Ohio State University (1972).

Career Highlights

- **Haile Selassie I University** 1958 to 1974 successively as: lecturer in education, Head of the Education Department, Dean of the Facilities of Arts and Education, Associate Academic Vice President and lastly as President of the University (1969-1974).
- **Sports and Youth Affairs in the Government of Ethiopia** (1974-1977) Minister of Culture.
- **UNICEF** Chief of the Education Division; and Special Advisor to the Executive Director (1990-1994).
- **World Bank** Director of the Education and Training Department (1977-1987)
  - Special Advisor to the Vice President of the Africa Region (1987- 1990)

In recognition of his contributions Dr. Aklilu Habte has been recognized and awarded numerous medals and certificates of honor from Ethiopia, France, the International Association of University Presidents and civic organizations.

Assefa Tsegaye
TMS Class of 1951

Assefa Tsegaye is a distinguished legal professional and banking executive whose career spans decades of influential roles in Ethiopia's financial and legal institutions. Born in Harar, he moved to Addis Ababa at a young age to study at TMS and went on to join the first group of 72 students at the University College of Addis Ababa when it opened in 1951. Ato Assefa's contributions to Ethiopia's banking sector include serving as the first Ethiopian Chief Legal Advisor, Deputy General Manager and Managing Director of the Commercial Bank of Ethiopia, followed by a pivotal role as Advisor and member of top management of the National Bank of Ethiopia. He later opted for early retirement and set up an office as a Consultant and Attorney at Law. His achievements have earned him high regard, including the naming of a Commercial Bank of Ethiopia branch in his honor, as well as a documentary on his life and legacy.

Education
- Law Diplomas, B.A., LL.B. Haile Selassie I University (1955; 1967; 1968;)
- Higher Banking Studies, England (1970)

Career Highlights
- **Board Member** — Oversight of several Ethiopian financial and industrial enterprises
- **National Bank of Ethiopia (Central Bank)** — Advisor (1977-1979)
- **Commercial Bank of Ethiopia** — Deputy General Manager; Managing Director (1973-1977), Legal Advisor (1967-1973), Senior Attorney and Assistant Legal Advisor (1965 — 1967)
- **State Bank of Ethiopia** — Legal Department
- **Ministry of Foreign Affairs** — Assistant to Directors-General of the American and Middle East Departments

Community Involvement
- **Consultant and Attorney at Law**

Assefa Tsegaye has rendered pro bono legal services and has actively participated in a number of philanthropic organizations free of charge.

Adam Abdallah, PhD
TMS Class of 1953

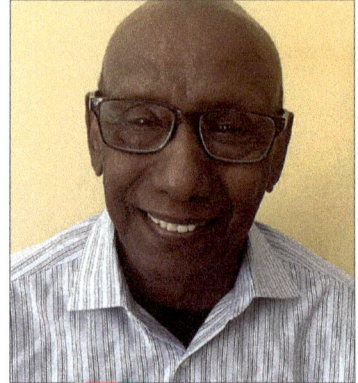

Dr. Adam Abdallah is an academic and higher education administrator with experience in the Ethiopian and
the United States school systems. Born in Dire Dawa,
he was a student at Quranic Islamic Arabic School until
he turned eight years old in 1945 when selected to be
among only nine students from his hometown granted
TMS scholarships by His Imperial Majesty Haile
Selassie I. Dr. Abdallah went on to build a career that
has similarly — and meaningfully — contributed to
the academic promise of new generations. In 1973, he was awarded a USAID scholarship to pursue his doctoral studies and, afterwards, continued his career in the U.S. until
retirement.

Education
- PhD in Education, University of Wisconsin, Madison, 1978
- Master of Education, Boston College, 1960
- BA in Education, *with distinction*, University College of Addis Ababa, 1957

Career Highlights
- **City University of New York (CUNY)** — Professor, Medgar Evers College; Higher
  Education Officer (1987-2007)
- **Founding Member and Vice President for Political Affairs** — Ethiopian Peoples'
  Democratic Alliance (1982-1986)
- **Education Programs and Research** — Various roles to direct higher education at
  Marquette University; University of Wisconsin; Director of Ethiopian Secondary
  School Leaving Certificate Examinations (1971-1981)
- **Haile Selassie I University** — Special Assistant to the Academic Vice President;
  Director (1968-1971)
- **Ministry of Education**-- Director General of Secondary Education; Director of
  Ethiopian Secondary School Leaving Certificate Examinations (1965-1968)
- **Harar Teacher Training Institute** — Director (1963-1965); Instructor, Education
  Psychology and Philosophy of Education (1960-1962)

Community Involvement
Director (Appointee), Prince Makonnen Haile Selassie Secondary School — new insti-
tution in hometown of Dire Dawa (1962-1963)
Founder and Chairman, Ethiopian Community Association of the Piedmont Triad in
North Carolina

Hailu Gebre Hiwot
TMS Class of 1953

Ninety-one-year-old Hailu Gebre Hiwot who first enrolled at Tafari Makonnen School as a day student in Grade 2 in 1945, has led a remarkable life as an accomplished economist and philanthropist. Among his many accomplishments is the discovery and trademarking of Yirgacheffe coffee, which has revolutionized Ethiopia's coffee industry and export landscape. Hailu now manages Kidane Mehret Students' Self-Help Association (KMSSA), an organization founded by his late wife that is committed to the education and wellbeing of students in Ethiopia.

Education
- MA in Economics — University of California, Berkeley (1960)
- BA in Economics, *with distinction* — Addis Ababa University (1958)

Career Highlights
- **Managing Director, KMSSA** — Providing education and social service support to students in need and establishing an academy to train the next generation of financial sector professionals (currently)
- **Investor, Share Dealing Group of Addis Ababa** — Pioneered Ethiopia's private investment sector through an initiative of the National Bank of Ethiopia
- **Innovator and Entrepreneur** — Established a diversified agricultural farming enterprise including discovering premier coffee brand Yirgacheffe
- **A. Besse & Co.** — First degreed Ethiopian to be hired by the company; provided managerial oversight of coffee production

Community Involvement
Hailu Gebre Hiwot is in the process of building an academy to provide advanced and specialized training for the financial sector of banking and insurance.

Major Hailemariam Abai
TMS Class of 1954

Born in 1937 in Adwa, Ethiopia, Major Hailemariam Abai began his education at the local church before gaining admission to TMS in Addis Ababa — a privilege granted due to his father's status as a Patriot from Adwa. A decorated public administrator and military officer, he held various leadership positions within the Ethiopian Armed Forces and government ministries. Later, he extended his expertise to development initiatives in Cameroon and the United States, contributing significantly to their progress.

Education
- Master of Public Administration, Syracuse University, New York
- BA in Public Administration, Addis Ababa University
- Basic Military Engineering, Kirkee, Poona, India
- Harar Military Academy, Ethiopia

Career Highlights
- **Humanitarian and Association Organizations** — Pan African Institute for Development in Cameroon and Council of Government of Washington, DC
- **Permanent Secretary** — Ministry of Coffee and Tea Development, Government of Ethiopia
- **Department Head** — Ministry of Interior, Government of Ethiopia
- **Awraja Governor** — Menagesha, Asosa Province, Wollega
- **Ethiopian Armed Forces** — Aide-de-camp to the Ground Force Commander; Aid to the Chief of Staff; Chief Administrative Officer to Chief of Staff Office

Community Involvement
Longtime member and former Board Member of Debre Genet Medhanealem Ethiopian Tewahido Church

Addis Anteneh Kassa
TMS Class of 1955

Addis Anteneh Kassa completed his elementary education in Gojjam and high school at Tafari Makonnen in
Addis Ababa in 1955. He is a seasoned economist with
decades of experience in agricultural economics, development planning, and international consulting. He has
played pivotal roles in notable Ethiopian and global institutions including as Board Chairman of the Bank of
Abyssinia, a premier private bank. (2002-2005)

Education
- M.Sc. in Agricultural Economics, University of Illinois (1961)
- B.A. in Economics, University College of Addis Ababa (1959)
- Economic Theory Credential, Economics Institute, University of Colorado (1959)
- Agricultural Project Analysis Credential, Economic Development Institute, World Bank (1969)

Career Highlights
- **Independent Economic Consultant** (1991-2012)
- **International Livestock Centre for Africa** — Senior Economist (1981-1991)
- Country Representative, ILCA, Gaborone, Botswana (1980-1981)
- **Government of Ethiopia:**
  - **1978 - 1979:** First Deputy Secretary-General, National Development Campaign and Central Planning Supreme Council, Addis Ababa.
  - **1975 - 1978:** Deputy Commissioner, Planning Commission, Ethiopian Government
  - **1971 - 1975:** Manager, Agriculture Dept., Agricultural and Industrial Development Bank, Addis Ababa.
  - **1968 - 1971:** Head, Planning Unit, Awash Valley Development Authority, Addis Ababa.
  - **1967- 1968:** Economic Expert, Prime Minister›s Office, Addis Ababa.
  - **1963 - 1967:** Economic Studies Section Head, Ministry of National Community Development, Addis Ababa.
  - **1961 -1963:** Junior Economist, Blue Nile Survey, Water Resources Dept., Ministry of Public Works, Ethiopian Government

Major Argaw Kabtamu
TMS Class of 1958

Major Argaw Kabtamu is a distinguished retired military officer and diplomat with a prestigious career spanning decades of service to Ethiopia. He is married, a proud father of three sons, and grandfather to four grandchildren. Born in Kimir Dingay (North Shoa), he was in fifth grade when he enrolled as a boarding student at TMS. Upon graduating in 1958, he was among four students selected to attend the newly established Haile Selassie 1st Military Academy in Harar where he went on to graduate with high rank and the academic credential-equivalent of two years of coursework at Addis Ababa University. Presented his diploma by His Imperial Majesty Haile Selassie I, Major Argaw proceeded to take on positions in military training, instruction, and security before assuming his first leadership role as Aide to the Deputy Chief of Staff.

Education

- Diploma in Military Science and Academics, rank of 2nd Lieutenant — Haile Selassie I Military Academy (1961)
- Advanced Infantry Leadership Training — Fort Benning, Georgia, USA (1969-1970)

Career Highlights

- **Entrepreneurship** — Co-founder, Board Member and Chairman, Yenegew Sew, Education Share Company
- **Diplomacy** — Various positions within the Ministry of Foreign Affairs including Head of North Africa and the Middle East; 1st Secretary; Acting Charge D`affaires; and founding member of The Intergovernmental Authority on Development (IGAD) for Eastern Africa.
- **Military and security service** — Aide to the Deputy Chief of Staff; Head of Training at Army Headquarters; Security Representative, Ethiopian Airlines (Paris); Military Academy Instructor

Artist Dr. Debebe Eshetu
TMS Class of 1958

Artist Dr. Debebe Eshetu is a pioneer in Ethiopian theater and operatic arts, known for his extensive contributions as an actor, writer, teacher, and advocate for cultural development. With over 40 stage plays, numerous films, and eight books, his work has elevated Ethiopian arts globally. He also served as a leader in international arts forums and as a champion for social causes, including peacebuilding and anti-HIV campaigns. The Addis Ababa University awarded Artist Debebe Eshetu an Honorary Doctorate for exemplary contributions to the arts (2023)

Education
- Theater and Operatic Arts Education, Haile Selassie I University (1963)
- Graduated from an art school in Hungary (1963)

Career Highlights
- **Performer** — Acted in over 40 stage plays and numerous international films, including 'Shaft in Africa'
- **Author** — Published eight books on Ethiopian arts and culture
- **Activist** — Advocacy for community development and peacebuilding through art
- **Elected Coordinator** — All-Africa by UNESCO Theater Institute (1983)
- **President** — African Performing Arts Association (1983)

Community Involvement
Artist Dr. Debebe serves on the Board of the TMS Alumni Association (TMSAA).

Taye-Brook Zerihoun
TMS Class of 1959

Taye-Brook Zerihoun is a seasoned diplomat with a distinguished career in global policy and international relations. Born in Harar and raised in Addis Ababa, he joined the Harar Military Academy from 1959 to 1962 and later served in the Ethiopian Defense Forces from 1963 to 1967. During his career of service, Taye-Brook went on to contribute significantly to global peace-building, conflict resolution, decolonization and anti-apartheid efforts holding worldwide posts with the United Nations for nearly 40 years from 1981 to 2018.

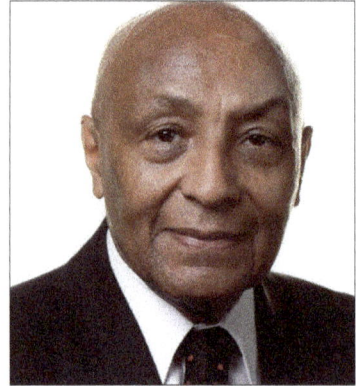

Education
- Master of Philosophy in Comparative Politics, Columbia University (1974-1977)
- MA in International Relations, Columbia University (1973-1974)
- BA in Economics, Columbia University (1969-1972)

Career Highlights
- Principal Deputy and Acting Head, UN Peacekeeping Mission in Sudan (2003-2007)
- Special Representative in Cyprus, United Nations (2008-2010)
- UN Assistant Secretary-General for Political Affairs, United Nations HQ (2010-2018)
- Joined the United Nations in New York in 1981 and worked initially in the decolonization and anti-Apartheid areas as well as on broader African issues, notably on conflict prevention and resolution.
- Policy Researcher, Center for Policy Research (1977-1980)

Tilahun Workeneh Eshetu
TMS Class of 1959

Tilahun Workeneh Eshetu was born in Debre Zeit and raised in Debre Sina and Addis Ababa, Ethiopia. He is a seasoned executive with extensive experience in agro industry, management consulting, and international trade. Starting his career in the sugar industry, Tilahun served in various roles of increasing responsibility, rising to Corporate Deputy General Manager after 27 years of stellar service at HVA Ethiopia before pursuing private industry and diplomatic posts. Tilahun has significantly contributed to trade and economic development in Ethiopia.

Education
- BA in Commerce, Haile Selassie I University (1964)

Career Highlights
- **Trade Commissioner** — Canadian Embassy in Ethiopia (1997-2013)
- **Partner and Senior Consultant** — Wass International, among the first private management consulting firms in Ethiopia (1991-1996)
- **Corporate Deputy General Manager** — Ethiopian Sugar Corporation formerly HVA Ethiopia (1964 — 1991)

Community Involvement
- Active in students' union at college.
- Fundraising to building an elementary school in Djeren, Djimma.
- Assisted in the establishment of the first Labor Union of Wonji/Shoa Sugar Factories.
- Managed a mobile school literacy program for shepherds in the surroundings of Addis Ababa.

Fekade Selassie Bezuneh
TMS Class of 1960

(In memoriam)

Fekade Selassie Bezuneh was a dedicated professional whose career spans decades of leadership in accounting, audit, and finance. Born in Debre Berhan, he completed his primary and secondary education at TMS. A scholar with a passion for service, Fekade left Ethiopia to pursue his undergraduate and advanced degrees, returning shortly thereafter in the early 1970s, intent on giving back to his country. He contributed significantly to the Ethiopia's financial institutions before political changes steered him back to the United States with his wife Rahel Asfaw, his high school sweetheart, and their two daughters. Over the course of his career, Fekade has held pivotal roles in private and public organizations, including PricewaterhouseCoopers (PwC), Coca-Cola, and the City of Atlanta. He was often celebrated for his commitment to his community, his family, and his profession.

Education
- Master's in Accounting, University of Minnesota, 1971
- Bachelor's in Business Administration, Bethune-Cookman College, 1969

Career Highlights
- **Private and public sector** — Chief Financial Officer, Lion's Group, an Ethiopian-owned firm in Atlanta; City of Atlanta; Coca-Cola Company
- **Financial services sector** — General Manager (Appointee), Ethiopia's Audit Service Corporation; PricewaterhouseCoopers (PwC) Philadelphia and Addis Ababa practices
- **Early career** — Ethiopian Airlines; Public Administration Institute

Community Involvement
Tafari Makonnen School Alumni Association; Member, First Board Election Committee

Tesfaye Aklilu, PhD
TMS Class of 1962

Born and raised in Addis Ababa, Ethiopia, Dr. Tesfaye Aklilu followed his father's and older brother's paths and attended Tafari Makonnen School from 1957 to 1962. A distinguished mechanical engineer and corporate leader, he has held senior positions at global corporations like Xerox and United Technologies. His expertise spans engineering, quality management, and operations research, impacting industries worldwide.

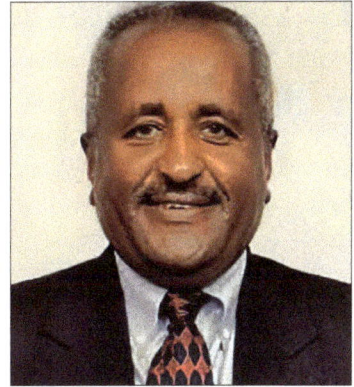

Education
- PhD in Operations Research, Oklahoma State University (1975)
- MSc in Mechanical Engineering, Oklahoma State University (1970)
- BSc in Mechanical Engineering, Oklahoma State University (1969)

Career Highlights
1970-1972 International Labor Organization
- Consultant

1976-1978 Babson College, Wellesley, Mass
- Taught Operations Research, Decision Theory, Simulation & Optimization

1978-1995 Xerox Corp
- Started as a Manufacturing Engineer and worked as Program Manager; Plant Manager; Information Manager; Marketing Manager and as Senior Executive.
- Vice President and Chief Information Officer, Office Document Division
- Vice President and General Manager, Document Production Division. Responsible for a $9 Billion Division

1995-2007 United Technologies Corp (UTC)
- **1995-1997** Vice President, Quality & Business Effectiveness, Pratt and Whitney, $21Billion (Aerospace Division of UTC)
- **1997-2000** Vice President, Quality, UTC, $60 Billion Aerospace and Building Business
- **2000-2007** Senior Vice President, UTC Manufacturing & Quality. Responsible for over 340 factories, 90,000 employees and over $35 Billion Budget

Yilma Kassaye
TMS Class of 1962

Yilma Kassaye is a successful executive with extensive experience in international trade. His leadership has spanned industries from agriculture to aviation, and his sharp business acumen has enabled his success both as an expert in the financial sector and as an entrepreneur. In addition to his business influence, Yilma's humanitarian work has also made an impact on society including through his efforts to mitigate widespread famine in Ethiopia.

Education
- BBA in Management with a minor in Accounting, Haile Selassie I University
- Advanced management trainings in London, Paris, and Berlin

Career Highlights
- **General Manager,** Zodiac Aviation Support, Inc. New York, NY 1996 — present)
- **President,** AGRIND American Trading, Inc. (1993 — present)
- **Commissioner,** Relief and Rehabilitation Commission (1990 — 1992)
- **General Manager,** Various enterprises including Yilge Agricultural Estate; Bishoftu Farms; Livestock Products Corporation; co-owned General Produce and Trading (1970-1979)
- **Head, Commercial Department**, Ministry of State Farms Development — Ethiopia (1980-1985)
- **Head, Ethiopian Trade Promotion Office** — Berlin (1985-1989)
- **Credit Officer,** Addis Ababa Bank (1967 — 1970)

Community Involvement
- Member of the Tafari Makonnen School Alumni Association

Daniel Jote Mesfin
TMS Class of 1963

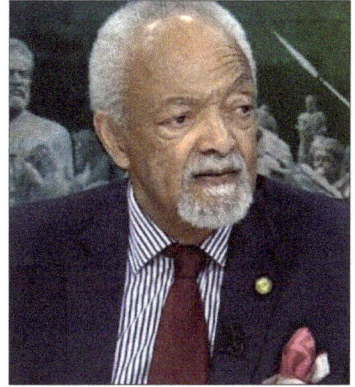

Daniel Jote Mesfin is a distinguished entrepreneur and advocate whose lifelong dedication to Ethiopia's growth, culture, and history exemplifies his unwavering commitment to serving his community and country. Educated in Ethiopia, the United Kingdom, and the United States, Daniel's celebrated career has spanned real estate, development, manufacturing, finance, marketing and publishing. His professional and personal achievements have positively impacted countless lives by bridging business and philanthropy to establish affordable housing, develop education programs, drive local tourism, build and renovate schools and churches, and as 10-year President of the Association of Ethiopian Patriots, champion veterans' welfare and the preservation of Ethiopia's history. Daniel recently edited the biography of his father Ras Mesfin Seleshi (Aba Tem Tem), which is being printed by University Press of Addis Ababa.

Education
- Bachelor's Degree in Economics, Marketing Minor, San Francisco State University
- Postgraduate Diploma in Agricultural Economics, Reading University

Career Highlights
- **Commercial Development** — Founder of enterprises that developed diverse properties ranging from affordable housing to the Babogaya Resort in Debrezeit Bishoftu
- **Publishing & Marketing** — Responsible for the publication and success of Ethiopia's first cookbook, selling over 40,000 copies globally, and the forthcoming release of Ras Mesfin Seleshi's biography
- **Philanthropy** — Established program for students to learn computer basics and programming
- **Leadership & Legacy** — Current President of the Association of Ethiopian Patriots, and 17-year member of fundraising committee, ensuring veterans' welfare and histor preservation including achieving national observance of Adwa Victory, Memorial Day, and Victory Day

Ayele Lemma
TMS Class of 1964

Ayele Lemma was born in Addis Ababa in 1948 and completed his elementary education at TMS, laying the foundation for a lifelong commitment to learning and leadership. He built a distinguished career as a dedicated administrator and educator making significant contributions across multiple industries, including engineering, agriculture, and academia.

Education
- BA in History *with distinction* — University of California, Berkeley (1976)
- MA in Career Management, John F. Kennedy University, School of Management (2011)

Career Highlights
- **Program Coordinator** — Part-time faculty, Berkeley City College (1990 — 2012)
- **Entrepreneur** — Management of family business (1988-1990)
- **Division Administrator** — Kaiser Engineers, Minerals Group (1978 — 1988)
- **Senior Secretary to FAO-UN Manager** — Agricultural Research Office (1968-1969)
- **Assistant Secretary to the Dean** — College of Engineering, Commercial School (1964 — 1968)

Community Involvement
- Highly creative fundraiser of TMS Alumni Association

Moges Gebremariam, MD
TMS Class of 1965

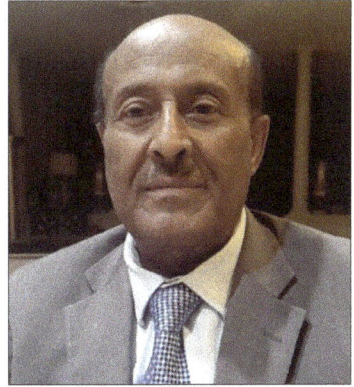

Dr. Moges Gebremariam is a highly accomplished physician, board-certified in internal medicine with a subspecialty in nephrology, with over four decades of experience in private practice, medical directorship, senior care and hospital affiliations. Born in Addis Ababa and educated at Haile Selassie I University, Dr. Gebremariam completed his medical training and residency in the United States. He has held leadership roles in multiple dialysis and advanced care facilities and continues his private medical practice today, alongside active participation in his community through contributions to philanthropic, faith-based and development efforts.

Education
- Diplomate (1981) and Board-eligible Nephrology Sub-Specialty (1982), American Board of Internal Medicine
- Nephrology Fellow, Maryland General Hospital, Nephrology (1977-1981)
- Chief Resident, Resident and Intern — St. Agnes Hospital (1972-1977) and St. Paul's Teaching Hospital (1971-1972)
- Doctor of Medicine, Haile Selassie University (1972)

Career Highlights
- **Private Practice** — Internal medicine, hypertension, and nephrology with several active professional memberships as well as hospital affiliations including Bon Secours, Sinai, and Maryland General (1981-present)
- **Medical Directorship and Attending Physician** — Dialysis facilities, nursing homes, and senior citizen centers (1991-present)
- **Staff Nephrologist and Physician** (1972-1990)

Community Involvement
Founding Member and Vice Chairman of Elders of Ethiopian Orthodox Church of Eyesus in Baltimore (1996-present); Ethiopia drought relief and water access campaign (2005); Cofounder of the TMS Alumni Association; Member, the TMS Centennial Committee, DMV Chapter; Member, The TMS Book Steering Committee.

Almaz Demisse
TMS Class of 1966

Almaz Demisse is a seasoned professional with a distinguished 42-year career at Ethiopian Airlines, during which she demonstrated exceptional leadership, versatility, and expertise across multiple disciplines. Beginning as a Typist Clerk in 1966, Almaz advanced to senior management positions with international scope, traveling extensively during her tenure with the company. Almaz's contributions spanned human resources, marketing, and management for existing and new station operations in Africa, Asia and Europe. Now retired, Almaz's legacy is a testament to her commitment to excellence in the aviation industry.

Education

- Advanced Secretarial Science Diploma, *with distinction* — Haile Selassie I University (1971)
- BA in Management and Administrative Science — Addis Ababa University (1983) Professional Certificates — Airline Marketing by Aer Lingus (1990); Basic Aviation Management (BAM) by International Aviation Management Training Institute of Canada (1990); Executive Development Seminar for Women Managers by Eastern and Southern African Management Institute, Nairobi, Kenya (1986); Earned 17 Certificate of Awards (1979 — 2000) for Airline related courses such as Leadership Skills, Managerial Effectiveness, Finance for non-Financial Managers, Decision-making,

Career Highlights
Ethiopian Airlines (1966-2008)

- **Management & Marketing** — Sales, marketing and cargo operations including representing company at conferences and exhibitions across Europe and Asia as Area Manager for China & the Pacific (1998 — 2005); Acting Director Cargo Marketing and Manager of Cargo Sales Development (1991 — 1994); Cargo Sales Programmer (1989-1991)
- **Human Resources** — Personnel operations and new station launch research as Manager, Employment (2006-2008) and Recruitment Officer (1982-1989)
- **Administration** — Assistant to Executive Secretary roles in support of personnel and operations departments (1966-1982)

Pankaj (PJ) Ratilal Kamani
TMS Class of 1966

Pankaj Ratilal Kamani, a multilingual financial expert and CEO, has a proven track record in creating, managing, and divesting successful businesses. While collaborating with financial institutions globally, he identified the need for high-quality translation and interpretation services for businesses and government agencies. In 1999, Pankaj founded ABC Language Services, assembling a skilled team capable of translating and interpreting in over 170 languages.

Education
- Harvard Business School, MBA in International Finance, Boston, MA 1976
- Haile Selassie I University, BBA in International Management • *cum laude*
- Successful completion of Hong Kong/Shanghai Bank's Credit Training program

Career Highlights
ABC Language Services (1999 — 2022)
- Founded and successfully grew a language services company translating in over 170 languages.

Alexander FX (formerly E. Alexander Co.), Hartford, CT (1996 — 2002)
- Managing Partner in a financial services company focused on investment banking.

AVFIN Resources, Cromwell, CT (1989 — Present)
- Vice President-- managed financial services for U.S. and international corporate entities and non-governmental agencies.

Hong Kong and Shanghai Banking Corporation (1983 — 1989)
- Vice President-- oversaw the marketing of financial services across multiple international markets.

The MEHTA Group, London, U.K. (1977 — 1983)
- Project Manager for diverse industrial investments in Africa, Middle East, and the U.K.
- Prior to MBA - served for 5 years as Purchasing Coordinator at **A. Besse & Co./EDISCO**, Addis Ababa, Ethiopia

Community Involvement
- Board Director, Pulmonary Fibrosis Foundation, 2021 — present
- Board Director, National Marrow Donor Program, Minneapolis 2012-2020
- Tetra State Chapter of TMS Centennial Committee

Petros Aklilu
TMS Class of 1966

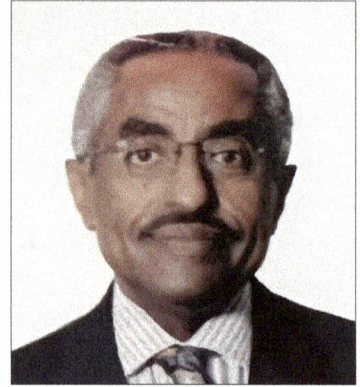

Petros Aklilu is a seasoned economist recognized for his pioneering work in rural development. With over three decades of experience advancing environmental and sustainable growth strategies, he has worked with the World Bank and United Nations amassing extensive regional expertise in East Asia, South Asia, Africa, Latin America, Eastern Europe, and the Middle East. A visionary, Petros has contributed to transformative initiatives, including establishing the Economic Analysis and Development Policy Unit at the UN World Food Programme (WFP) and chairing donor steering committees for dryland management in the Middle East and North Africa (MENA).

Education

- Executive Development Program, Harvard Business School, Harvard University (2003)
- Diploma in Development Economics, Cambridge University (1976)
- Master of Science in Agricultural Economics, University of Massachusetts (1973)
- Bachelor of Science in Economics, Oklahoma State University (1971)
- Haile Selassie I University, Addis Ababa (1969)

Career Highlights

- **Advisor** — Independent Evaluation Group, World Bank (2006-2007)
- **Chief** — Economic Analysis and Development Policy Unit, UN WFP (2004-2006)
- **Sector Manager** — Rural Development, Water, Environment, and Social Group, MENA Region, World Bank (1999-2004)
- **Senior Economist** — Various roles focused on agriculture, rural development, operations and human resources across Asia, South Asia, and the Middle East (1977-1999)

Community Involvement

- Founder and First Board President, Tafari Makonnen School Alumni Association in North America; now globally known as TMS Alumni Association (TMSAA)
- Founded a non-profit organization — "Community Development and Oral History." Helping rural communities gain access to primary education and clean drinking water.

Temesgen Petros
TMS Class of 1966

Temesgen Petros is a financial expert with decades of experience in grant management and community service. An alumnus of Howard University and the University of the District of Columbia, he served 38 years at the National Caucus and Center on Black Aging, rising to the executive post of Financial Controller. Temesgen is also the founder of a charitable foundation that supports disadvantaged students in the US and Ethiopia, in memory of his eldest son Yonathan.

Education
- BA in Finance and Economics, University of the District of Columbia (1975)
- BA in Accounting, University of the District of Columbia (1980)
- MBA, Howard University (1987)
- Haile Selassie I University business management coursework (1969-1971)
- Certified Insurance Producer, Real Estate Agent, and Microsoft Systems Engineer

Career Highlights
- **Founder,** Yonathan Foundation — Supports disadvantaged children and food-insecure individuals in the U.S. and Ethiopia (2019-present)
- **Financial Controller**, National Caucus and Center on Black Aging — Oversaw federal grant funds in positions of increasing responsibility for nearly twenty years until retirement (1982 — 2019)
- **Property Clerk**, Imperial Board of Telecommunications (1968 — 1971)

Community Involvement
- Served as Treasurer of Tafari Makonnen School Alumni Association in North America 1914-2020

Bisrat Aklilu, PhD
TMS Class of 1967

Dr. Bisrat Aklilu is a development economist with over 30 years of experience contributing to sustainable development, governance, and operations. He has held key leadership roles with notable institutions, including the United Nations Office for Project Services (UNOPS) and the United Nations Development Program (UNDP). Dr. Aklilu has continued to lend his expertise to fostering global development and peacebuilding. He served as a Goodwill Ambassador for Ecuador's Yasuni ITT Initiative, economics professor at Boston University, and is an active board member and adviser to several institutions.

Education
- Ph.D. in Economics, Boston University (1975)
- M.Sc. in Agricultural Economics, University of Massachusetts (1972)
- B.A. in Economics and Political Science, magna cum laude, Carleton College (1971)

Career Highlights
- Advisory Board Member, Global Alliance for a Sustainable Planet (2021-present)
- Senior Advisor, Syria Recovery Trust Fund (2013-present)
- Vice-Chair, Board of Directors, Chemonics International (2016-2023)
- Board Member, Oxfam America (2020-2023)
- Executive Coordinator, Multi-Partner Trust Fund Office, UNDP (2004-2013)
- Deputy Executive Director & Director of Operations, UNOPS
- Division Chief, IFAD Programme, UNOPS
- Senior Country Portfolio Manager, Africa and Near East Divisions, IFAD

Community Involvement
- **Co-founder and Board President, Tafari Makonnen School Alumni Association (TMSAA).**
- **Board Member, Ethiopian Diaspora Trust Fund — (2018-2020).**
- **Board Member, NY Tri-State Grand Ethiopian Renaissance Dam (GERD) Support, Inc.**

Fantu Cheru, PhD
TMS Class of 1967

Dr. Fantu Cheru is a Senior Researcher, African Studies Centre, Leiden University (The Netherlands) and Associate Senior Fellow at the Stockholm International Peace Research Institute (SIPRI). He served on the UN Secretary-General Kofi Annan's Panel on Mobilizing International Support for the New Partnership for African Development. He was Convener of the Global Economic Agenda Track of the Helsinki Process on Globalization and Democracy.

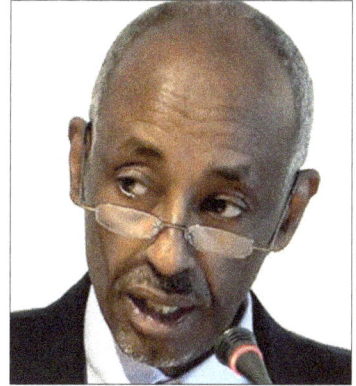

Career Highlights
- UN's Special Rapporteur on Foreign Debt and Structural Adjustment for the UN Commission for Human Rights in Geneva.
- Advisor and consultant to various governments and institutions, including the UNECA, UNDP, UN-Habitat, SIDA, DANIDA, and NORAD.

Selected publications:
- Agricultural Development and Food Security in Africa:
- The Impact of Chinese, Indian and Brazilian Investments (2013);
- Co-edited, Africa and International Relations in the 21st Century, co-edited
- The Rise of China and India in Africa (2010);
- African Renaissance: Roadmaps to the Challenge of Globalization (2002);
- Ethiopia: Options for Rural Development (1990);
- The Silent Revolution in Africa: Debt, Development and Democracy (1989);
- The Oxford Handbook on the Ethiopian Economy, 2019, with Arkebe Oqubay and Chris Cramer, Oxford University Press;

Community Involvement
- Chair, TMS Alumni Association European Chapter;
- Board Member, Center for Development, Research and Dialogue, Addis Ababa, Ethiopia;
- Founding Member, China-in-Africa, Adeica-IN-China
- Former Chair, the Africa Peace building Network, Social Science Research Council, New York.

Fikremariam Tsehai
TMS Class of 1967

Fikremariam Tsehai has dedicated over three decades to international development. His career spans roles in the Ethiopian Ministry of Foreign Affairs and global humanitarian organizations, including his impactful work with Canadian Lutheran World Relief, aiding in the resettlement of thousands of refugees. He has been honored for his incredible contributions to society with prestigious awards including the Human Rights Award by MOSAIC and the Global Advocacy Award by Wilfrid Laurier University.

Education

- DEA and Doctorat de 3ème cycle advanced degrees in Political Sociology from University of Paris
- BA from Haile Selassie I University

Career Highlights

- **Adjunct Professor** — University of British Columbia (1993 — 1996)
- **Head of Neighbouring Countries Department** — Ethiopian Ministry of Foreign Affairs (1977)
- **Diplomat** — Ethiopian Embassy in Paris and Permanent Mission to the UN in Geneva
- **Canadian Lutheran World Relief** — Led efforts to resettle over 10,000 refugees (1993-present)
- **Chair, Overseas Protection and Resettlement Working Group** — Canadian Council for Refugees
- **Recipient, Human Rights Award** (2016) and **Global Advocacy Award** (2024)

Hilletework Mathias, PhD
TMS Class of 1967

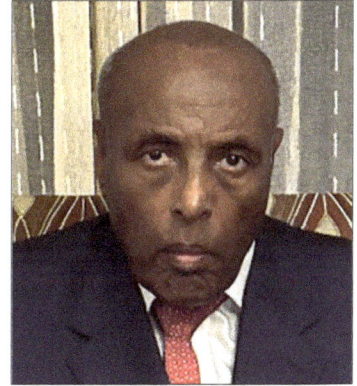

Dr. Hilletework Mathias is a passionate journalist and academic whose work has elevated global and African political issues. Spending decades at Voice of America and contributing to the integrity of international broadcasting, Hilletework has produced programming on a wide range of topics, from civil wars and national elections to natural disasters and health crises. Traveling extensively on assignment, his reports have included interviews with heads of state, senior officials, regional experts, and African scholars.

Education

- Ph.D. in African Studies, Howard University (1985)
- M.A. in Media Studies, American University (1977)
- B.A. in Broadcast Journalism, American University (1974)

Career Highlights

- **Program Analyst, U.S. International Bureau of Broadcasting** — Conducted program audits to strengthen quality, audience appeal, impartiality and integrity of international news (2005-2014)

- **Radio Broadcaster and Newswriter, Voice of America (VOA)** — Covered broad range of topics including reporting from war-torn Somalia during Operation Restore Hope and the subsequent Somali Peace Conference, and landmark political events such as Kenya's first multi-party elections in 1993 and Ghana's Economic Reform Program in 1999

- **Recognized with VOA Excellence in Programming Award** — Presidential Transition of Power (1990); Transition of Power During the Ethiopian Peace Talks (1991); Eritrean Referendum (1993); African Child Soldiers (1997); Islam in Africa (1997)

- **Research Assistant, Traffic World,** conducted thorough research on logistics news for modes of transportation magazine (1980-84)

Professor Meskerem Melke Tadesse
TMS Class of 1968

Meskerem Tadesse is a Tenured Assoc. Professor of Business Administration at the University of the West — receiving "The Most Outstanding Faculty Award" (2013 and 2018). She is a former Fortune 500 corporate executive with a broadly diversified career that spans 20 years and 4 continents. Her proprietary "Optimize-U Entrepreneurship Strategic Management" workshop series was adopted by Southern California Edison, one of the world's prominent utility companies. Meskerem was a Keynote speaker at the 2019 "ET-2050 International Conference" held in Addis Ababa. She has served on the Boards of Directors of multiple non-profit and corporate entities. She is a recipient of several awards such as the "Distinguished Leadership Award" from California Regional Black Chamber of Commerce.

Education
- University of Pittsburgh, Pennsylvania
  - B.Sc. in Management (1978)
  - MBA Finance & Marketing, KATZ Graduate School of Business (1979

Career Highlights
- 1979-85; **MOBAY, Chemical Corp.** , U.S. Sub. of BAYER AG, Germany
- 1985-2009: **CHRYSLER Corp.** — international Finance, Treasury Operations & FX Management
- 1994 - **Meski's Modes Internationale** — Owner/Designer, high-end Ethiopian boutique, Detroit, MI
- 2003 — **The Optimize Group, Inc.**, Founder/CEO — Strategic & Financial Management Consulting firm
- 2007 — Current: **University of the West**, Rosemead, CA-- Faculty, Business Admin. Director, Center for Minority and Small Business, and Editor of "The REVIEW" 2013-21
- 2019 - Visiting Professor, **St. Mary University**. Addis Ababa, Ethiopia

Community Involvement
- 1976: Executive Board Member, Ethiopian National Committee for International Women's Year
- Advisory Board Member, CSUDH Innovation Incubator
- TMSAA South California Chapter and Member of TMSAA Book Steering Committee

Abebe Abraham Joteh
TMS Class of 1968

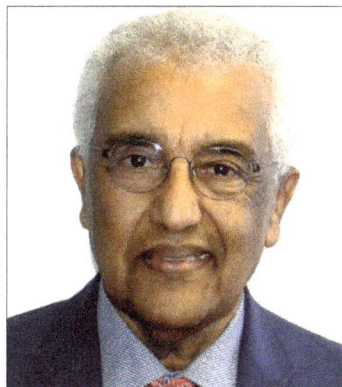

Abebe Abraham Joteh is a distinguished entrepreneur and business leader with extensive experience in marketing and management. As the founder of CMI Management, Inc. in 1986, he successfully led the company for 38 years, driving its growth into a nationally recognized full-service management firm. Under his leadership, CMI secured a $400 million federal contract — the largest small business award of its time. The company, which employed over 1,300 people across all 48 contiguous states, specializes in facilities management, logistics, records management, and administrative support services for both government and commercial clients. CMI has earned numerous accolades, including recognition as one of the *Washington Business Journal's* Top 100 Largest Private Companies and *Government Security News'* Top 100 DHS Contractors.

Education
- MBA in Business Administration, Northwest Missouri State University (1975)
- BS in Social Science, Baldwin-Wallace College (1972)

Career Highlights
- **Founder, President, and CEO** — CMI Management, Inc. (1986-2024)
- **Vice President of Industry Services** — BOMA International (1978-1986)
- **Merchandising / Marketing Manager** — Better Homes & Gardens (1976-1977)
- **Author of popular Small Business Book**, "*Thinking Your Way Out of the Ditch*" (2016)

Community Involvement
- Cofounder and active member, Tafari Makonnen School Alumni Association (TMSAA)
- Contributor: *Tafari Makonnen School: Inspiring Lives of Achievement Since 1925*
- Member: Board of Deacons, Assembly of God International Church
- Translation: *The Words of Jesus* into Amharic, an Ethiopian National Language.

Garedew Atnaf-Seged
TMS Class of 1968

Garedew Atnaf-Seged is a notable professional with over three decades of experience in the automotive industry. He is also a successful entrepreneur with ventures in hospitality and retail. Following his memorable time at TMS, Garedew pursued his higher education in the United States. A graduate of Youngstown State University, he earned a bachelor's degree in business administration while working part-time on the assembly line at General Motors (GM) — where he would later go on to build a long and rewarding career after graduation. His first full-time position at GM was in accounting. He continued to advance to more senior positions in quality control management and even operational supervision of the assembly lines he once worked as a student. After retiring from GM in 2005, Garedew and his family settled in Maryland where he pursued entrepreneurial interests. He opened a convenience store and managed a family restaurant started by his wife of 43 years, Senedu Zewdie, with whom he shares two children.

Education
- Bachelor's in Business Administration, Youngstown State University, 1972

Career Highlights
- **General Motors** — A 33-year career spanning finance, management, quality control, and assembly operations in positions of increasing leadership and technical and business acumen (1972-2005)
- **Entrepreneurship** — Hospitality and retail ventures

Community Involvement
- Tafari Makonnen School Alumni Association (TMSAA) Board Member since 2016

Merafe Seyoum
TMS Class of 1968

Merafe Seyoum is a seasoned professional with a rich history of leadership and service in posts across Ethiopia, Germany, and the United States. She credits her formative years at TMS with instilling the confidence and discipline necessary to pursue higher education and professional excellence. Over her career, Merafe has served in key roles for the Ethiopian Ministry of Finance, Addis Ababa University, and the United Nations, where she worked in the accounting department until her retirement in 2017. Beyond her professional endeavors, she is a dedicated community servant, contributing to both Ethiopia- and U.S.-based women's associations, credit unions, churches, and Edirs. Since 2018, Merafe has proudly served as Treasurer of the Board for the TMSAA. She currently resides in New York with her husband and four sons.

Education
- Bachelor's in Accounting, Addis Ababa University

Career Highlights
- Accounting — United Nations
- Various positions — Addis Ababa University
- Secretary, Legal Department — Ministry of Finance, Government of Ethiopia

Community Involvement
- Treasurer, Board of Directors — Tafari Makonnen Alumni Association (2018-present)

Yemesrach Felleke Eregetu
TMS Class of 1968

Yemesrach Felleke Eregetu is an accomplished professional and entrepreneur with a career spanning insurance, international relations, and community service. Her educational journey began at Licee Gebre-Mariam, continued at Nazareth School and, later, she joined the Commercial Section of TMS. After furthering her education in the United States, Yemesrach returned to Ethiopia to launch her career and dedicated over two decades to the Ethiopian Insurance Corporation. She also contributed to the industry by supporting the establishment of the Association of Ethiopian Insurers before founding her own enterprise, Shebelle Ethiopia Conference Services, together with her late husband Yohannes Kifle. Yemesrach has demonstrated a deep commitment to community service as a lifelong volunteer for the Ethiopian Orthodox Church and as Chairperson of the TMSAA Ethiopia Chapter.

Education
- Addis Ababa University
- American Field Service Programs — Narbonne High School, Milpitas, California

Career Highlights
- **Shebelle Ethiopia Conference Services** — Co-founder, Co-owner, Deputy Managing Director
- **Association of Ethiopian Insurers** — Liaison Officer and Secretary to the Executive Board
- **Ethiopian Insurance Corporation** — Various managerial roles over 23 years
- **Canadian Embassy** — Secretary to the Administrative Officer

Community Involvement
- Member, Tafari Makonnen School Centennial Committee

Amha Mersie Hazen
TMS Class of 1969

Amha Mersie Hazen is an economist and seasoned management consultant, fluent in five languages. With decades of experience, Amha has built a notable career working for renowned institutions while also publishing the historical works of his legendary father who was one of the first educators at TMS when the school opened in 1924.

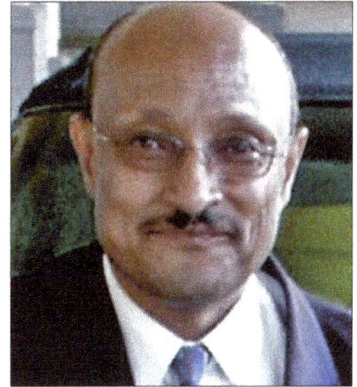

Education
- M.S. in Economics, Purdue University, Indiana (1977)
- B.S. Equivalent, Cyril & Methodius University, Skopje, Yugoslavia (1974)

Career Highlights
- **Management Consultant** — Ernst & Young, World Bank, UN Habitat, Umgeni Water, South Africa and others.
- **Procurement and Contract Administration** — various management positions in local and regional government, U.S.
- **Editor and Publisher** — Issued award-winning book 'Yehayagnaw Kifle Zemen Mebacha' and six additional works of his father and respected historian Blatta Mersie Hazen

Community Involvement
- One of the founders of the Ethiopian Community Center in Portland, Oregon
- Active member of the Tafari Makonnen School Alumni Association (TMSAA)
- Co-chair and contributor, Steering Committee of TMS Centennial Book.

Berhan Dargie
TMS Class of 1969

Berhan Dargie is an accomplished legal professional, dedicated to public service, with extensive experience spanning Ethiopia and the United States. After earning an LLB from Haile Selassie I University, he began his legal career at the Ethiopian Highway Authority, eventually managing its Legal Services Division. In the United States, Berhan continued his education at Howard University Law School, earning an LLM, and has since built a successful legal practice specializing in personal injury law in Washington, DC.

Education
- Master of Law (LL.M), Howard University Law School, 1996
- Bachelor of Laws (LL.B.), Haile Selassie I University, Law School, 1980
- District of Columbia Bar Association, Admitted 1997

Career Highlights
- **Private Practice**, Washington, DC (1997-present)
- **Legal Assistant**, Washington, DC (1989-1995)
- **Ethiopian Highway Authority** — Various positions advancing to Legal Services Division Manager (1977-1988)

Community Involvement
- The Law Office of Berhan Dargie in Washington, DC generously provides TMS Alumni Association (TMSAA) with full access to essential office resources, enabling seamless operations. In addition to offering a dedicated workspace, Berhan Dargie, cofounder and the first Board Secretary of TMSAA, also serves as the organization's trusted legal advisor, ensuring compliance and guidance through legal matters with his expertise.

Tadesse Goshime
TMS Class of 1969

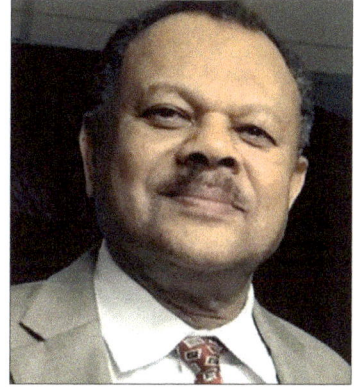

Tadesse Goshime is an accomplished educator with over two decades of experience teaching mathematics at the secondary and collegiate levels. After starting his career in technology manufacturing, Tadesse went on to spend more than 20 years teaching the next generation of innovators in metropolitan school districts in Pennsylvania and Maryland before retiring in 2019. His expertise spans classroom instruction, curriculum design, and student mentorship across diverse educational settings, delivering engaging instruction and fostering critical thinking in mathematics.

Education
- MS, Instructional Science, Mathematics
- Teaching Certificate, Mathematics (Grades 7-12), Maryland & Pennsylvania
- BA, Public Administration
- Diploma, Field Services and Computer Technology

Career Highlights
- **Mathematics Teacher** — Montgomery County Public Schools (2003-2019)
- **Lecturer** — Montgomery College (2007, 2008, 2014)
- **Mathematics Teacher** — School District of Philadelphia (1998-2003)
- **Adjunct Math Professor** — Temple University (2002)
- **Manufacturing Head, ESD** — Led operations for manufacturing of smart card control units (1996-1998)
- **Field Service, Video and Audio Equipment** — Thorn Services (1992-1996)
- **Project Manager and Field Technician** — Logic Electronics (1989-1992)
- **Head, Administration Department** — Berta Construction (1977-1982)

Community Involvement
- Member of TMS Centennial Committee — DMV Chapter

Alem W/Hawariat Mathias
TMS Class of 1970

Born and raised in Ethiopia, Alem began her educational journey at Nativity Girls School in Addis Ababa and transferred to Tafari Makonnen School in the ninth grade graduating in 1970. She joined Haile Selassie I University in 1970 and relocated to the United States in 1971 where she earned her B.S. degree in Business Administration and held pivotal roles in a Fortune 500 company of freight railroads and resorts for nearly 30 years.

Education

- Bachelor of Science in Business Administration, *magna cum laude* — Bowie State College (1975).
- Corporate-sponsored professional training in Business Writing, Management, US Legislative Process, Federal and State Election Campaign Laws, and Political Action Committees (PACs) in Washington, DC (1980-90's)

Career Highlights
CSX Corporation — 1976-2005

- Director of Political Affairs — 2002-2005
  - Manager, Public Affairs & Affiliated PACs 1997-2001
  - Administrator & Treasurer, CSX Political Action Committee (PAC) 1993-1996
  - Manager, Government Relations Department (double role)
  - Administrative support to Senior VP; Office Manager 1976-1992
  - Recipient, Corporate Masters Award — CSX's highest employee recognition (1992)
  - Assigned staff, The Private Sector Survey on Cost Control Project — Commissioned by President Ronald Reagan (1985)
- **Entrepreneur** — 1985-2013
  - Established small businesses in retail, consulting and real estate management.

Community Involvement

- Tafari Makonnen School Alumni Association (TMSAA), Board VP
- DGMA Ethiopian Orthodox Church Fundraising Committee

Captain Kebede Woldetsadik
TMS Class of 1970

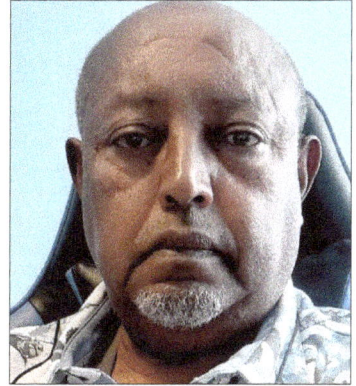

Born and raised in Addis Ababa, Captain Kebede Woldetsadik is a distinguished aviation professional who built an illustrious career over four decades with Ethiopian Airlines. Starting as a First Officer with the country's only national airline in 1974, Kebede progressed to Captain, flying advanced aircrafts such as the Boeing 777 and 787 Dreamliner, before retiring in 2017. Committed to supporting public service, Captain Kebede donates his time to volunteer initiatives that give back to his community and country, including serving as a Board Member of the TMSAA.

Education
- Ethiopian Airlines Pilot Training Program, 1974
- Tafari Makonnen School, Class of 1970
- President, Current Events Club, Tafari Makonnen School, 1970
- Ongoing aviation industry training and compulsory certifications

Career Highlights
- Ethiopian Airlines — Advanced from entry-level First Officer on DC-3 aircraft through the ranks until elevated to Captain B-777/B-787 (1974-2017)
- Head of Flight Operations (1998-2002); cabin crew and cockpit crew were under flight operations by then.

Community Involvement
- Board of Directors — Tafari Makonnen School Alumni Association (TMSAA)
- TMS Centennial Committee Ethiopia Chapter

Artist Lulseged Retta
TMS Class of 1971

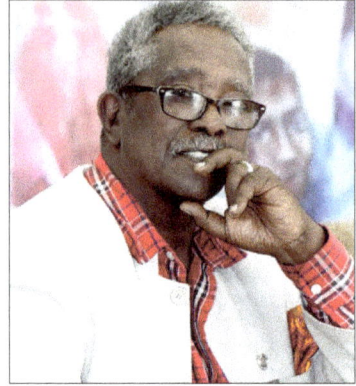

Lulseged Retta is a renowned Ethiopian artist, born and raised in Addis Ababa. He graduated from Tafari Makonnen School in 1970 and pursued his passion for art in work that blends traditional Ethiopian art with modern techniques, reflecting his philosophical and African motifs. Lulseged's artistry, international recognition, and community contributions make him a prominent figure in Ethiopian and global art scenes. In recognition of his exceptional contributions, he was recently awarded a medal by the Prime Minister of Ethiopia Dr. Abiy Ahmed.

Education
- Addis Ababa School of Fine Arts 1977
- MFA from the Repin Academy of Arts, Leningrad (St. Petersburg) 1986 (with great distinction)

Career Highlights
- Former civil servant at Ethiopia's Ministry of Culture and Information and Tourism Commission.
- Extensive solo and group exhibitions since 1982 across Ethiopia, Djibouti, Kenya, Cairo, South Africa, Mali, Zimbabwe, Russia, China, Japan, United States, Canada, Geneva, Germany.
- Featured in notable publications: Who's Who in International Art (1994-95) and catalogs for prestigious exhibitions-- The Osaka Triennale (1996) and Cairo Biennial (1998-99).
- Cofounder and participant "Art of Ethiopia"; an annual event organized at The Sheraton Addis Luxury collection.
- Runs a private studio in Addis Ababa and is a Fellow of Ethiopian Studies at Addis Ababa University.

Community Involvement
- Board Member of Tafari Makonnen School Alumni Association (TMSAA)
- Member, TMS Centennial Committee Ethiopia Chapter
- Member of Rotary International and Rotary club of Addis Ababa West

Selamawit Yisma
TMS Class of 1971

Selamawit (Selam) Yisma is a highly skilled procurement and administrative professional with extensive experience supporting nonprofit organizations, international development initiatives and peacekeeping missions. She has a stellar track record for streamlining procurement processes, standardizing contracts, building collaborative stakeholder relationships and liaising with high-ranking officials, having launched and implemented hundreds of successful programs that uplift underserved communities while meeting high organizational efficiency standards.

Education
- New York University, Robert F. Wagner Graduate School of Public Service
- MPA in Public & Nonprofit
- Addis Ababa University, BA in Public Administration
- United Nations Development Program (UNDP), Certificate / Procurement

Career Highlights
- **United Nations** (ECA, UN Headquarters and Peacekeeping Missions: Namibia, Kuwait and ex-Yugoslavia: Croatia); United Nations Development Program; Procurement, Administrative Associate and Office Manager (1975-2005)
- **UNDP, Multi-Partner Trust Fund Office** -- Provided high-level administrative support to the Executive Coordinator, a fund administrator of United Nations system with $5.4 billion portfolio. Liaised with high-level Government/Senior International Officials with tact, confidentiality and great team spirit. (2007-2011)

Community Involvement
- **Tafari Makonnen Alumni Association** (TMSAA), Board Member since 2014
- **All Star Projects**, a nonprofit organization that helps transform the lives of youth and poor communities using the developmental power of performance in its afterschool programs
- **America SCORES**, A nonprofit organization that inspires urban youth to lead healthy lives, be engaged students, and have the confidence and character to make a difference in the world.

Haile Assegide
TMS Class of 1972

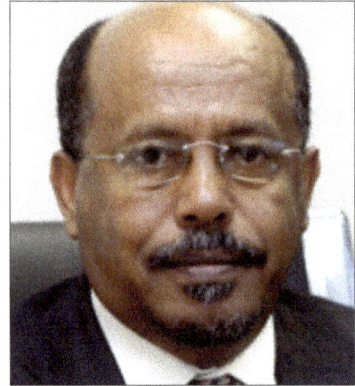

Haile Assegide, an accomplished leader committed to Ethiopia's national development, is the Chief Executive Officer of Derba MIDROC Cement Plc and Derba Group in Addis Ababa where he was born and raised. Haile has played a pivotal role in advancing Ethiopia's infrastructure and industrial sectors. He has lent his engineering and executive management expertise to prestigious organizations such as the Ethiopian Roads Authority; Ethiopian Electric Power Authority; Ethiopian Telecommunication Authority; Construction Business Bank; Ethiopian Airlines; Ethiopian Airlines Restructure Project (Chair); Addis Ababa University; Ethiopian Standard Authority; Ethiopian Investment Authority; Dashen Bank S.C; and Sandford International School.

Education

- M.Sc. in Construction Management, Loughborough University of Technology, UK, 1991
- B.Sc. in Civil Engineering, Haile Selassie I University, 1978

Career Highlights

- **CEO, Derba MIDROC Cement Plc and Derba Group** — Leading Ethiopia's premier cement production company and driving industrial innovation (2005-present)
- **State Minister, Ministry of Infrastructure** — Oversaw national infrastructure development projects (2000-2005)
- **Minister, Ministry of Construction and Urban Development** — Spearheaded urban development and construction policies (1992-2000)
- **Ethiopian Water Works Construction Authority** — Held various roles including Chief Engineer and Project Manager for major water supply initiatives (1983-1992)
- **Project Engineer** — Held various roles in rural and urban development at Norwegian Save the Children (1981-1983) and Berta Construction (1978-1981), including contributing to the Ambo Water Supply Project

Abebe Zegeye, PhD
TMS Class of 1973

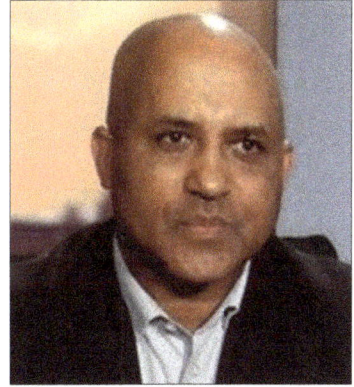

Dr. Abebe Zegeye, a distinguished scholar and author, has dedicated his career to the study of African and social identities. Among his numerous publications is the acclaimed book "The Impossible Return: The Beta Israel of Ethiopia," which is being translated into Arabic. Over the course of his extensive career in academia, Dr. Abebe has held prestigious positions in research, instruction, and institutional leadership. Currently, he serves as Co-Director of Cradle: Center for Research and Training in Addis Ababa, Ethiopia, and as Adjunct Professor of Political Science at Bahir Dar University. As further seen through his community involvement work with South African History Online and contributions to policy initiatives under the South African President's Office, Dr. Abebe's passion and legacy continue to shape African scholarship and institutional development.

Education
- Doctor of Philosophy, University of Oxford (1985)
- Bachelor of Arts in Economics, Philosophy, and Sociology, Haverford College, Pennsylvania (1979)

Career Highlights
- **Co-Director, Cradle: Center for Research and Training** — Addis Ababa (present)
- **Various professorships and prestigious administration positions** — Bahir Dar University (present), Ethiopia; Woldia University, Ethiopia (2016-2019); Wollo University, Ethiopia (2014-2015); Yale University, USA (2008-2009); University of California, Santa Barbara, USA (1995-1998)
- **Ministry of Science and Higher Education** — Director of Global Engagement & Institutional Transformation; Director Higher Education
- **Primedia Chair of Holocaust and Genocide Studies** — University of South Africa

Azeb Asrat Hailemariam
TMS Class of 1973

Azeb Asrat Hailemariam is a dedicated leader with over three decades of professional experience in food security and international development, and a passionate advocate for humanitarian efforts. Through her 28-year career with the United Nations World Food Programme (WFP) and Food and Agriculture Organization (FAO), Azeb was involved in policy advisory, project management and review. As an active Rotarian since 2013, she has held numerous key leadership roles most recently from 2022 to 2023 as Governor for Rotary District 9212, overseeing activities in Eritrea, Ethiopia, Kenya, and South Sudan.

Education
- Bachelor's in Personnel Management and Administrative Sciences, Addis Ababa University
- Advanced training in senior leadership, monitoring and evaluation, conflict resolution, and project management

Career Highlights
- **Board Service, Rotary Club** — Various posts and appointments including Club Trainer (2021-present); District Governor (2022-2023); Country Chair and Vice Chair of the Ethiopia Board (2018-2023); President and Treasurer of the Rotary Club of Addis Ababa West (2015-2018)
- **UN WFP** — Deputy Country Director in Sri Lanka and Sudan (2006-2012); Senior Regional Programme Advisor in East, Central and Southern African Countries (2001-2006); Regional Programme Coordinator in South East Asian Countries (1998-2001); Emergency Coordinator in Bosnia Hercegovina (1996-1998); Project Officer in Ethiopia (1986-1993)
- **UN FAO** — Various administrative and senior secretarial positions (1984-1986)

Community Involvement
- TMS Centennial Committee, Ethiopia Chapter; Member of TMSAA Book Steering Committee;
- Motivational speaker; mentor; empowers youth and inspires audiences on important topics including leadership and career development.

Getachew Tesfaye
TMS Class of 1973

Getachew Tesfaye is a distinguished engineer specializing in nuclear power, with over four decades of experience. He has held international roles in nuclear reactor design, project management, and regulatory oversight. A former player for Ethiopia's first division club, Getachew's love of soccer inspired him to bring the Ethiopian Sport Federation to North America as a founding member, also going on to serve a six-year term as federation president.

Education
- M.S. in Mechanical Engineering — Massachusetts Institute of Technology (MIT)
- B.S. in Mechanical Engineering, *summa cum laude* — Howard University

Career Highlights
- **Lead Project Manager, U.S. Nuclear Regulatory Commission** — Evolutionary power reactor and small modular reactor design (present)
- **Technical Secretariat, OECD-NEA, Paris** — Generation III and IV reactors
- **Nuclear Power Plant Engineer** — Implementing operational safety and efficiency at power plants in the U.S.
- **Nuclear Power Plant Designer** — Combustion Engineering and IMPELL Corporation

Community Involvement
- Chairman, TMS Centennial Committee DMV Chapter
- Ethiopian Soccer Federation in North America

Konjit Tedla Haile
TMS Class of 1973

Konjit Tedla Haile has had an extensive career with Ethiopian Airlines spanning roles across key operational areas including human resources management, regional sales and operations, and brand visibility and advertising. With over four decades of experience and achievement, her dedication to operational excellence, stakeholder engagement and talent development has left a lasting impact on the airline industry.

Education
- BA in Management and Public Administration, Addis Ababa University (1986)

Career Highlights
- **Head of Advertising and Sales Promotions**, Ethiopian Airlines (2016-2018)
- **Director of Sales for Greater China, Mongolia and North Korea**, Ethiopian Airlines (2012-2016)
- **Regional Manager for Kenya and Seychelles,** Ethiopian Airlines (2007-2012)
- **Acting Vice President, Human Resource Management,** Ethiopian Airlines (2003-2007)
- **Programming, administration and personnel management** — Various positions, Ethiopian Airlines (1976-2003)

Community Involvement
- Konjit Tedla serves as Secretary of the Board and Country Representative of the TMS Alumni Association
- Member, TMS Centennial Committee — Ethiopia Chapter

Nardos Bekele-Thomas
TMS Class of 1973

H.E. Nardos Bekele-Thomas is the first woman to lead the African Union Development Agency (AUDA-NEPAD). Appointed as Chief Executive Officer in 2022, she has championed sustainable development across Africa, emphasizing regional integration and human development. With a distinguished career at the UN, she has held leadership roles in South Africa, Kenya, and Benin, promoting trade and investment. Her interest includes advancing human development anchored on the principles of economic, social and political rights for all.

Education
Master's degree in Economic Development, Monetary Economics, and Econometrics from New York University

Career Highlights
- **Chief Executive Officer -- African Union Development Agency -NEPAD** — Driving Africa's Agenda 2063 (present)
- **Senior Director** — Office of UN Secretary-General Ban Ki-Moon
- **UN Resident Coordinator** and UNDP Resident Representative in Benin
- **UN Resident Coordinator** and UNDP Resident Representative in Kenya
- **UN Resident Coordinator in South Africa**
- **Deputy Resident Representative** — UNDP Kenya
- **UNDP Private Sector Policy Advisor on Africa**

Community Involvement
- An accomplished bilingual author in French and English, Mrs. Bekele-Thomas was also honored by the African Union alongside several woman presidents and first ladies.

Mohammed Kamil Sherif, MD, DIH, FRIPH
TMS Class of 1974

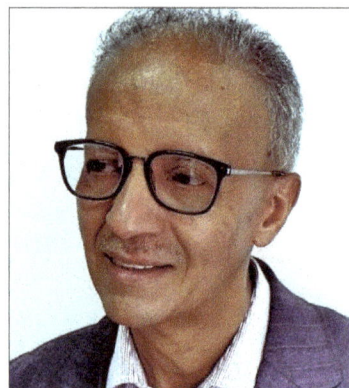

Dr. Mohammed Kamil Sherif is an accomplished medical professional with over four decades of experience in healthcare leadership, public health, and clinical medicine. Born in Addis Ababa, Dr. Sherif has held high-level hospital administration, primary care, and family medicine roles across Ethiopia and Botswana, overseeing hospital operations and improving patient outcomes. Since 2000, he has been the Medical Director of Central Medical Centre in Palapye, Botswana and further contributes to community health initiatives and healthcare delivery as a member of renowned professional organizations like the International AIDS Society and the World Organization of National Colleges and Academies of Family Physicians. Dr. Sherif is married with three children and fluent in English, Arabic, Aderegna, and Amharic.

Education

- M.D. — Addis Ababa University (1982)
- Pre-medical Sciences — Addis Ababa University (1978)
- International Fellowships — Royal College of Physicians & Surgeons, Ireland; Royal Academy of Medicine, Ireland; Royal Institute of Public Health and Hygiene, London

Career Highlights

- **Medical Director** — Central Medical Centre in Palapye, Botswana (2000-present); Shashamene General Hospital, Ethiopia (1984-1986); Woldia Hospital, Ethiopia (1983-1984)
- **Principal Medical Officer In-Charge** — Thamaga Primary Hospital, Bostwana (1999-2000); Palapye Primary Hospital, Bostwana (1995-1998)
- **Senior Medical Officer In-Charge** — Palapye Primary Hospital, Botswana (1989-1994)
- **Medical Officer In-Charge** — Tsabong Primary Hospital, Botswana (1987-1989)
- **Ethiopian National Service (1975-1976)**

Fasil Giorghis
TMS Class of 1980

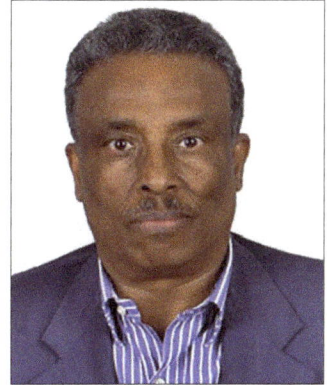

Fasil Giorghis is an accomplished architect, urban planner and heritage conservator. Born in Gondar, he began his educational journey at Debreselam Catholic Mission before moving to Addis Ababa where he later graduated TMS in 1980. Currently an associate professor at the Ethiopian Institute of Architecture, Building Construction and City Development (EIABC), he leads the Master's program in conservation. Through his private firm, Fasil Giorghis Consult, Fasil has played a pivotal role in shaping Ethiopia's architectural heritage, blending modern design with historical preservation.

Education
- Master's in Architecture, Helsinki University of Technology, 1990
- Bachelor of Science in Architecture, Addis Ababa University, 1985

Career Highlights
Addis Ababa University (1985-present)
- Chair, Conservation of Urban and Architectural Heritage (2010-present)
- Associate Professor, EIABC (2012-present)
- Chair, Department of Architecture (1996-1998)
- Lecturer, Architecture (1990-2011) and Graduate Assistant (1985-1988)

Founder and Principal Architect, Fasil Giorghis Consult (1996-present)
- Expertise in architectural and landscape design, urban planning and conservation with notable works including the Red Terror Memorial Museum; additions to the historic Alliance Ethio-Francaise; restorations of Saint Mary's of Tsion Church in Axum, Goethe Institute, Holy Trinity Cathedral and National Palace

Community Involvement
- Founding Member — Association of Ethiopian Architects; Ethiopian Heritage Trust
- President — ICOMOS Ethiopia (present); NESTOWN Ethiopia (past)
- Fellow — Ethiopian Academy of Sciences

Tarik Teferi
TMS Class of 1982

Born and raised in Addis Ababa, Tarik attended Mekane Eyesus School before transferring to TMS in 1976 where she completed 12th grade in 1980 and later joined the evening program of commercial studies, graduating in 1982. Tarik worked at the Ethiopian National Television as a continuity live host in 1983 before moving to the United States where she has built an impressive 35-year career at Cigna Global Healthcare Insurance Company, holding various roles that showcase her adaptability and leadership. Now residing in Dallas Metroplex in Texas, Tarik is married and has one adult daughter.

Education
- Certified Maxwell Leadership Coach, Trainer and Public Speaker
- Computer Science, Napa Valley College

Career Highlights

Cigna Global Healthcare Insurance Company
- **Network Adequacy Provision Team** — One of six employees (among 70,000) maintaining operational excellence
- **New Hire Trainer**
- **Team Leader**
- **Utilization Management** — Through Intra Corp., Cigna sister company
- **Assistant to Network Medical Doctors** — Workers Compensation Division
- **Front Office Receptionist** — Through Cigna-owned doctor offices

Community Involvement
- Tarik is deeply engaged in her community through the Ethiopian Community Radio, Kidmia LeLejochachen Saturday Amharic School, and the Ethiopian Women Organization. She is also a founder of the Agape Global Leadership Council.
- Member, TMSAA Texas Chapter; TMS Centennial Committee

Mehrteab Leul Kokeb
TMS Class of 1985

Mehrteab Leul Kokeb, a senior law professional with 25 years of experience specializes in corporate and transactional law. He is currently practicing at Mehrteab & Getu Associates (MLA) in Addis Ababa and manages a diverse range of cases, including contractual disputes, arbitration, unlawful competition, liquidations, and employment matters. Proficient in delivering comprehensive legal services to individual and corporate clients, he excels in trials, mediations, motion practice, depositions, and document preparation. Known for his analytical skills and exceptional oratory, Mehrteab is adept at navigating complex legal cases and achieving favorable outcomes. He has also gained specialized training on public-private partnerships and energy projects through the African Development Bank.

Education
- Master of Laws in Commercial and Corporate Law, University of London (2021)
- Postgraduate Diploma in Laws, Corporate and Securities Law, University of London
- Postgraduate Certificate in Financial Services Law, University of London (2019)
- Bachelor of Laws (LL.B.), Addis Ababa University (1992)
- Leadership training, Harvard Business School (2024)

Career Highlights
- Corporate law — Developed strategies for corporate growth, including country-specific business plans for General Electric and Coca Cola in Ethiopia
- High-profile cases — Played a pivotal role in a high court case, private equity transactions, and corporate registrations, demonstrating expertise in managing complex legal and business challenges
- Financial sector — Advised on critical financial deals involving Exim Bank of China and China Development Bank, including sovereign debt arrangements, cross-border pipeline financing, and regulatory compliance

Getaw Worku Hassen, MD, PhD
TMS Class of 1988

Dr. Getaw Worku Hassen was born and raised in Addis Ababa. He has over 24 years of experience as a practicing physician in New York and has held several leadership roles in emergency medicine and research. In addition, as an educator and mentor dedicated to future generations of medical professionals, he has been recognized with multiple awards for excellence in teaching.

Education
- Residency in Emergency Medicine, New York Medical College (NYMC), 2010
- Surgical Intern, Maimonides Medical Center, 2007
- Ph.D. in Neural and Behavioral Science, SUNY Downstate Medical Center, 2006
- M.D., Johannes Gutenberg University, Mainz, Germany, 2000

Career Highlights
- **Professor** — Department of Emergency Medicine (DEM), NYMC (2016 — present)
- **Committee Member** — Tenure, Appointments and Promotion Committee, NYMC (2023-present)
- **Attending Physician** — DEM, Columbia University Medical Center (2018 — present)
- **Attending Physician, Director of Research, and 3D-printed Simulation Director** — DEM, Metropolitan Hospital Center (2010-present)
- **Attending Physician** — DEM, NYU Langone-Brooklyn (2010-2018)
- **Medical Director** — RJ Medical and Urgent Care (2016-2018)
- **Clinical Instructor, Dept. of Neurology** and Consultant for Center for Drug Delivery and Research — SUNY Downstate Medical Center (2006-2012)

Community Involvement
- President, Wegen Le Wegen (2021-2022)
- Led NY-based nonprofit supporting commitments in Ethiopia
- COVID-19 Response
- Delivered medical aid and devices to hospitals and displaced groups
- American College of Emergency Physicians--Ambassador to Ethiopia
- Conducts annual workshops, mentors physicians, and supports medical innovation

Tsigereda Tafesse Mulugeta
TMS Class of 1995

Tsigereda Tafesse Mulugeta is a public policy expert with over 17 years' experience in urban management, policy advising, and capacity development. A graduate of the University of London, she has contributed to development cooperation and led large-scale research projects across multiple African nations. Tsigereda is currently the Country Coordinator for Cities Alliance focused on Ethiopia and Somalia and previously served as an adviser to the third First Lady of Ethiopia.

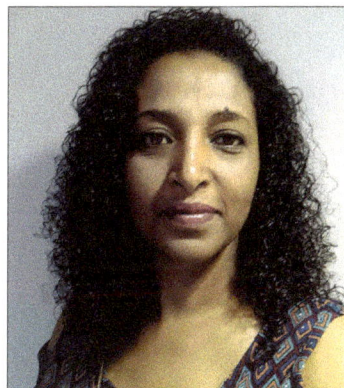

Education
- MSc in Public Policy and Management, University of London
- Center for Financial and Management Studies
- BA in Sociology and Social Administration, Addis Ababa University, College of Social Science
- Certified Capacity Works Facilitator, Deutsche Gesellschaft für Internationale Zusammenarbeit (GIZ)

Career Highlights
- **Country Coordinator, Cities Alliance** — Ethiopia and Somalia migration and sustainable urbanization (current)
- **Advisor to First Lady of the Democratic Republic of Ethiopia** (2016 — 2018)
- **Senior Policy Advisor, GIZ** — Urban development and establishment of Ethiopian Cities Association and Ethiopian Cities' Week
- **Freelance consultant** — New York University advisor on 30-year African urban expansion plans; Ethiopian Diaspora Trust Fund manager of project grant systems; Conference and meeting planner including Colours of the Nile Film Festival

Community Involvement
- Served as Secretary and Country Representative of Tafari Makonnen School Alumni Association
- Member, TMS Centennial Committee — Ethiopia Chapter

On behalf of the Board of Directors of the Tafari Makonnen School Alumni Association, I am pleased to express our deep appreciation to former EPTC/TMPTC Dean Teshome Feissa and current EPTC/TMPTC Dean Abdulber Mohammed Nasir whose professional profiles follow. Their enthusiastic and creative collaboration and steadfast support have been invaluable in forging the close partnership between TMSAA and the College and in developing TMSAA's assistance program, including the exciting Center of Excellence "TMSAA Building" that will be built on the TMPTC campus. Dean Teshome has been a steadfast advocate in the restoration of the illustrious name Tafari Makonnen to our beloved school.

Bisrat Aklilu, President
Board of Directors
Tafari Makonnen School
Alumni Association (TMSAA)

Abdulber Mohammed Nasir
Dean, EPTC / former TMS

Dean Abdulber Mohammed Nasir has built a distinguished career in education, leadership, and research, primarily focusing on improving educational institutions and administrative structures in Ethiopia.

Education
- Diploma in Chemistry (2003-2004) Kotebe Teachers Training College
- B.A. in Chemistry (2005-2008) Addis Ababa University (AAU)
- B.A in Information Communication Technology (2006-2009) AAU
- M.A. in Educational Leadership (Planning & Management) (2011-2012) AAU

Career Highlights
Educational Policy and Supervision (2024-current):
Dean, EPTC, former TMS
- Manages technical and vocational education programs; staff recruitment, curriculum innovation, and institutional growth.
- Oversees integration of technology and software management into academic administration and continues to conduct action research to improve educational methodologies and student outcomes.

Addis Ababa Administration Educational Bureau (2023-2024)
Supervisor Directorate — Supervised schools, ensured curriculum adherence, and developed strategic policies for improving education quality across multiple institutions.
- Educational Research and School Administration (2012-2023)
- Ginbot 20 Secondary & Preparatory School (2008-2012 E.C) served as Principal, managing academic programs, student affairs, and institutional development
- Vice Director at Atse Zerayakob Primary & Secondary School (2008-2009); contributed to school administration, curriculum implementation, and teacher supervision.
- Chemistry Teacher at Hiber Primary School (2004-2007) in Nifas Silk Lafto sub-city.

Community Involvement
- Involved in building partnerships between schools and local communities to enhance educational support structures. Promotes equity and inclusion in academic institutions.

Teshome Feissa
Former Dean /EPTC

Born in Addis Ababa, Ethiopia, Teshome Feissa Waktola is an accomplished educator and administrator who brings extensive expertise in Information and Communications Technology (ICT). Recognized for his leadership and innovative solutions, he is dedicated to advancing the Technical and Vocational Education and Training (TVET) sector.

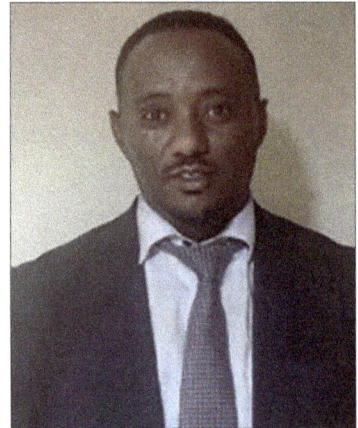

Education

- MA Degree in TVET Leadership & Management; Federal TVET Institute (2024)
- BSc in Information Systems; Addis Ababa University (2007)
- Diploma in English Language Teaching; Kotebe Teachers College (2006)
- Level IV Certification in Hotel Operations; Ibex Hotel & Tourism Management College (2013)

Career Highlights
Dean, EPTC, former TMS (2022-2024)

- Administered outcome-based training, staff development, and strategic planning to deliver quality education.
- Managed competency assessments.
- Teamed up with international stakeholders: the Technical University of Munich and GIZ.
- Focused on leadership that emphasized capacity-building, organizational development, and fostering collaborations between academia and industry.

Vice Dean, Addis Ababa Tegbar-id Polytechnic College (AATPTC) (2019-2021)
Institutional Capacity & International Relations Vice Dean, AAPTC (2017-2019)
ICT Trainer and Department Head of ICT -- AATPTC (2014-2017)

- Supervised digitalization initiatives, developed HRM systems and trained more than 650 graduates in digital and soft skills.
- Planned and organized workshops for delivering quality training
- Managed the international relationships of the College
- Provided consultancy services for trainees and support to other private and non-government TVET training institutions/colleges, trainees and industry.
- Capacitated the skills and knowledge of the trainers.

Community Involvement

- Building a network infrastructure in collaboration with KOICA as a professional volunteer in Berhan Ethiopia

Chapter Three

Creation and Growth of the Tafari Makonnen School Alumni Association (TMSAA): Alumni Response to TMS Founder's Adera (Solemn Plea)

Bisrat Aklilu, Contributor

TMS Class of 1967

President of the Tafari Makonnen
School Alumni Association (TMSAA)

Creation and Growth of the Tafari Makonnen School Alumni Association (TMSAA):

Alumni Response to TMS Founder's Adera (Solemn Plea)

Introduction

Before discussing how the Tafari Makonnen School Alumni Association (TMSAA) started, its purposes, accomplishments and challenges, we must first consider why we need an alumni association. What is the purpose and objective of an alumni association, particularly in a country like Ethiopia, where there is no tradition of alumni associations?

There are two reasons for providing a comprehensive account of how TMSAA started and progressed over the years. First, the current TMSAA members of about 600 alumni represent only a tiny fraction of the total number of students who graduated from TMS or its predecessors. As a result, most TMS alumni are unaware of the objectives, accomplishments, and challenges of TMSAA and TMSAANA. As TMSAA expands globally and new members join the Board, it is essential to put on record and document the evolution, successes, and challenges of TMSAA.

Second, since the concept of an alumni association is not well established in Ethiopia, it is crucial to motivate and encourage alumni of TMS, as well as those of other high schools in Ethiopia, to form similar associations that can support their alma maters and current students. As is well-known globally, high schools, colleges, and universities greatly benefit from the support of their alumni, both financially and substantively. Therefore, it is essential to firmly establish, promote, and encourage a culture of "giving back to one's school and community" in Ethiopia.

During the last few years, I have received messages from several formal or informal alumni organizations in Ethiopia (or established abroad) who are interested in learning about the experiences of TMSAA, often requesting assistance to help them establish their alumni organizations. Out of these organizations, I am pleased to see the Shimeles Habte School Alumni Association in North America (SHSAANA) and የ Lycée ልኜ-Lycée Guebre Mariam Alumni Association are well established and growing.

This section will first present a chronological development of TMSAANA, the Addis-based short-lived Tafari Makonnen School Charity Alumni Association (TMSCA) and TMSAA, focusing on the biannual TMSAANA and TMSAA General Assembly meetings and the various TMSAANA and TMSAA Boards. It will present the significant activities undertaken by TMSAANA and TMSAA and their accomplishments over the years. It concludes with the key lessons and challenges TMSAANA and TMSAA face, which are likely to be faced by other alumni associations that have recently begun operations. If these challenges are not adequately addressed and resolved, they will pose a significant risk for the future of TMSAA, which can reverse the many positive results and accomplishments achieved with hard work and sacrifice.

One of the main goals of TMSAANA, TMSACA, and TMSAA is the historical correction of the illegal, unjustified, and anti-Ethiopian history decision of the military dictatorship (the Derg) by restoring the century-old name of Tafari Makonnen School (TMS for short) from the Derg given Entoto Comprehensive School. In the current context, this means replacing the Entoto Polyethnic College (EPTC) with Tafari Makonnen Polytechnic College (TMPTC).

In this section, I refer to Entoto College as Tafari Makonnen (TMS), even though I wrote this chapter before the TMS name had been officially restored. This is because of the widespread and almost universal reference of the College by Addis Ababa residents, if not all Ethiopians, as TMS. When asked where they go to school, it is striking how even the current students of EPTC unanimously mention TMS and not EPTC. Similarly, when taxi or bus drivers are asked to drive towards EPTC, they automatically ask, "You mean Tafari Makonnen?"

I was fortunate to get my elementary and secondary education at TMS. A public school where students from all walks of life, with different socio-economic, ethnic, and religious backgrounds, join the school after passing a 'fit to be a good student' aptitude test if not a formal entrance test. In my case, as my three elder siblings were studying at TMS and our father was also among the first students of TMS when it opened up in 1917, it was a relatively straightforward process to get accepted at TMS. I never thought of going to any other school besides TMS as soon as I got old enough to walk 3 km from our house to TMS. After spending my first two school years, grades one and two, at our neighborhood Patriots School, I joined TMS, which was overwhelming in size, about 137,000 square meters, and had a vast student body of more than 1,000 at that time.

In addition to an excellent education, TMS introduced me to many sports (baseball and basketball) and extracurricular activities. During our student years at TMS, students joined groups or teams to enjoy activities or discuss issues of common interest. Among the most popular of such groups were the Scout Club, the Theatre Club, the Debating Club, the Current Events Club and the Radio Club, all except the Scout Club I actively participated in. These activities expanded my horizons and built my self-esteem. Seeing TMS teachers who came from various countries and helped us excel in our education instilled a strong desire to get involved in public service when I grew up. That is when I first met Mr. Doug Eadie, our English and history teacher, as we called him then.

When I reached the 11th grade, following in my older brother's footsteps, I applied for and succeeded in being selected to join the American Field Service (AFS) program. AFS was a program that gave students the opportunity to live for one year with an American family and attend a senior year at an American high school. Doug Eadie was the AFS advisor who interviewed students and recommended their participation in the program.

In my case, I went from sunny Addis Ababa to attend Minnetonka Senior High, in a suburb of Minneapolis, Minnesota, where the temperature from December to March is freezing — from -10 to -15 centigrade. During my AFS year, I did exceptionally well in my studies. To the surprise of my American teachers, who initially thought I would find it challenging to take senior class courses, I realized what an excellent education I had received at TMS.

During high school graduation, we were all recommended to join the Minnetonka High School Alumni Association and keep in contact with each other and the school. That was my first introduction to an alumni association. Similarly, following my graduation from Carleton College (BA degree) and later Boston University (MA and PhD), I began receiving regular requests to donate as an alumnus of these schools. Since I received a scholarship to attend these universities, it was natural to feel duty-bound to give back whatever I can to show my gratitude for my free education.

It was clear that alumni associations bring former students together to create a sense of community and fellowship. They are also a significant source of funding and support to their alma maters and help alumni find jobs after graduation. Alumni also provide strategic advice to their schools and allow them to know the outside world's demands regarding strategic investments and program development.

The practice of alumni helping their alma mater reminds us of Ras Tafari Makonnen's following famous words to TMS students on April 27, 1925, when TMS was inaugurated, what TMS alumni regularly recall as the "Adera" or "Solemn Plea," and has become TMSAA's guiding motto.

> This school is an instrument which will operate on our country's be-half through the knowledge which God gives to each of you accord-ing to your lot, once you have matured in wisdom and have become vigorous in intelligence. So I beg of you to help the school which nurtures you, and gives you the food of knowledge: to see that it does not shrink but expands, to see that it does not fall but grows in strength.
>
> **Regent Ras Tafari Makonnen's April 27, 1925,**
> **Inaugural Speech for Tafari Makonnen School**

The official and legally incorporated Tafari Makonnen Alumni Association, known as Tafari Makonnen School Alumni Association in North America (TMSAANA), started in 2011, followed by the current global Tafari Makonnen School Alumni Association (TMSAA) in 2021. However, the first effort to set up an alumni associa-tion was made by a group of TMS alumni eleven years earlier in 2000 during the preparation to celebrate the 75th TMS Anniversary.

TMS 75th Anniversary Alumni Committee

In 1999, alumnus Tafesse Bogale, class of 1974, mobilized his close colleagues to plan the celebration of the 75th TMS Anniversary on April 27, 2000 (Ethiopian calendar, 19 Miazia 1992). A TMS 75th Anniversary Committee, pictured below,[1] including sub-committees dealing with Fund Mobilization, Finance, Public Relations, and Documentation, was formed.

On Saturday, April 8, 2000, a fundraising dinner was held at the Sheraton Hotel in Addis Ababa. As the event was widely announced on radio and television, it was well attended by alumni, past and present teachers, and friends of TMS. The two well-known Artists and TMS alumni, Debebe Eshetu and the late Haimanot Alemu were the hosts of the dinner event.

For the occasion, a 75th Anniversary magazine was published in May 2000 by a publication committee comprising Amha Mersie Hazen,

75th TMS Anniversary Committee[1]

Girma Feissa, Dawit Kassa, Tadesse Meshesha, and Tsega Selassie Mitku. The magazine acknowledged the 75 Anniversary Committee's aim of using the occasion to help the school to form a Tafari Makonnen Alumni Association (TMSAA).

---

1 Members of the Committee were: Seated from left to right, Elias Meshesha, Dawit Kassa, Gezhagne Tegegne, Tadesse Meshesha, Tafesse Bogale; 2nd row, from left to right, Marta Habetemariam, Atnafu Negash, Dereje Worku, Teshome Gebre Mariam, Mesfin Belay, Teklemariam Zemichael, Abebe Biru, Kebede Getahun; 3rd row, from left to right, Meskerem Adefris, Gebre Egzabher Kidane, Girma Feissa, Demissie Abebe, Tedla Makonnen, Negatu W/Yohannes, Amha Mersie Hazen and Almaz Kebede. Not in the picture are Tesfaye Gessese, Nigatu Taye, Haimanot Alemu, Debebe Eshetu, and Aselefech Mulugeta

One of the articles in the 75th Anniversary magazine was titled "Tafari Makonnen Tomorrow?" and clearly shows how TMS alumni intended to form a Tafari Makonnen School Alumni Association:

> What should be our vision of the TMS of tomorrow? To answer this question, it is important to recall what the long-time TMS Assistant Director, Mr. Marcel Gagnon said: *"You the lucky TMS alumni who are alive, have the responsibility to reestablish the name and fame of TMS. Because you are the outcome of TMS."*
>
> Yes, we must give back to TMS. This is why we are planning to establish a Tafari Makonnen School Alumni Association; form a provisional ad hoc committee; undertake various activities to meet the legal requirement for the association's establishment; finalize alumni member registration; and soon call a provisional alumni association general assembly where the association's Board members will be elected and take charge of the alumni association.
>
> In performing this noble task, we are very confident that TMS alumni who are abroad will support us by providing advice, finance, and material contributions. What alumni abroad have already done gives us great confidence as they have already provided TMS with computers and means to expand internet connections. As a result, useful connections have been established. Continuation and strengthening of this partnership require the effort of all parties.

Towards the establishment of an alumni association, several alumni and some organizations, who are listed in the 75th Anniversary magazine, gave financial donations.

Unfortunately, the provisional alumni committee did not proceed with officially establishing and legally registering a TMS alumni association. Nevertheless, it conducted considerable lobbying with government authorities to restore the TMS name. An alumnus who was a member of the provisional alumni committee[2] reported that the committee made a request to the late Prime Minister Meles Zenawi, through the then Speaker of the House, Dawit Yohannes, a TMS alumnus, for the TMS name restoration. The Prime Minister apparently indicated he has no issue with the name

---

2 Note I received from Captain Yegzeru Belete, class of 1974, about the 75th Anniversary Celebration

restoration; however, he referred it to the Mayor of Addis Ababa, who has official oversight of the school. The Mayor of the time is said to have declined the request for the name change.

The Committee searched in many places to locate the bust of the Emperor that used to stand in the center of the "Church building" and was removed from TMS by the Derge. It found the bust in the basement of the National Museum, where many statues and carvings of the imperial era had been discarded. The Emperor's bust was damaged, but the committee had it repaired, painted in gold, and returned to its former place, where it remains to this day.

The Emperor's Bust, Restored

In addition, in consultation with some government officials, the committee removed the gypsum that covered the TMS name on the entrance of the main building. These are two iconic artifacts that evoke fond memories of the TMS years of any TMS alumnus.

The TMS Name at the Entrance of the Main Building

As the 75th Anniversary Committee did not have a legal basis for its official continuation, its activities were limited after the 75th Anniversary. Some members continued to meet unofficially, though they did not establish a formal relationship among themselves, with the TMS administration or TMS students, which gradually led to the disbanding of the group.

The Tafari Makonnen School Alumni Association in North America (TMSAANA)

Eleven years later, my brother, alumnus Petros Aklilu, class of 1966, initiated the establishment of the first legal TMS alumni association — the Tafari Makonnen School Alumni Association in North America (TMSAANA), the predecessor to the current Tafari Makonnen School Alumni Association (TMSAA). According to Petros, the Founding President of the first TMSAANA Board of Directors, the establishment of TMSAANA arose from a conversation he had with our mother in 2010. He informed her about the decline in the quality of education at TMS since our school days in the 1960s, noting that TMS had lost its former prestige. She challenged him to rectify the situation, reminding him that "your father, you, and your brothers all attended TMS," urging him to take it upon himself to help his former school.

Petros decided to meet the challenge and called a meeting of TMS alumni in Addis Ababa in mid-November 2010. With the assistance of the then Dean of Entoto Technical and Vocational Training College (ETVTC), formerly TMS, a meeting of TMS alumni was arranged. About 30 alumni, primarily graduates of the 1950s and 1960s, attended the meeting. He urged the alumni to establish an association in Ethiopia, explaining that he would do the same upon returning to the US, a proposal the alumni enthusiastically agreed to.

Upon his return to the US in November 2010, he contacted his longtime TMS classmates. He briefed them about his meeting with the alumni in Addis and the necessity of establishing a TMS alumni association in the US. They all agreed to the idea and decided to create a website to register alumni in the US and Canada. In March 2011, with the support of a volunteer friend of Yirgu Wolde, the first alumni website, https://www.ourtms.com, was designed and launched, and alumni registration commenced.

Simultaneously, an alumni bylaws drafting Committee comprising the late Fekade Bezuneh (class of '60), Yafet Tekle ('66), Yirgu Wolde ('66), and Petros Aklilu

('66) articulated the objectives and operational provisions of the association. The draft bylaws were reviewed and finalized by alumnus Berhan Dargie ('69), an attorney in Washington, D.C., who has continued to provide TMSAA with legal advice and the use of his office as TMSAA's legal address.

The founding alumni's vision for the new association was the restoration of the TMS name, the upgrading of the quality of the College's education, and the promotion of the high-quality education we had experienced at TMS, both in the classroom and through our participation in sports and extracurricular activities. They rightly believed that restoring TMS's former glory would produce high-caliber graduates and cultivate good citizens who would serve their communities and country. Their objective is aligned with the vision of TMS's founder, Ras Tafari Makonnen, as articulated in his often-quoted inaugural speech of April 27, 1925, which Doug Eadie referenced in the opening pages of Chapter One and I cited earlier in this chapter.

The drafting committee postponed the presentation of the draft bylaws to alumni until the number of registered alumni reached at least 50. Since TMSAANA's membership reached 87 by July 31, 2011, the Committee conducted the bylaws approval vote on August 14, 2011. Fifty-seven alumni, or 66% of the registered alumni, approved the bylaws, which became effective.

To expedite the election of the first Board of Directors, the committee drafting the bylaws established a Board Election Committee comprising members from diverse geographic areas. Accordingly, alumni Fekade Selassie Bezuneh ('60) from Georgia served as Chair, along with Alem W. Mathias ('70) from Virginia, Zewdie Hailu ('66) from Minnesota, and Yafet Tekle ('66) from California, who were designated as the Board Election Committee.

The Founding and First TMSAANA Board of Directors: November 2011 - October 2014 and First TMSAANA Biennial General Assembly, May 2012

On November 21, 2011, the TMSAANA members unanimously approved the Election Committee's recommendation to appoint the following alumni as the first Founding Board of Directors:

1- Petros Aklilu — President
2- Yirgu Wolde — Vice President
3- Tsehay Elias — Treasurer
4- Berhan Dargie — Secretary
5- Henock Gugsa — Web Administrator

The main challenges facing the first Board of Directors were getting the large pool of TMS alumni in North America to join TMSAANA and thereafter getting them to donate funds for start-up activities and pay the annual membership payment. The annual payment was initially set at only US $20 until December 2012 and increased to US 120 per year starting 2013. This payment challenge continued to affect TMSAA until 2023 (see Table 8).

Following the Washington, DC, government's issuance of a Certificate of Incorporation as a non-profit organization, TMSAANA received a Federal Tax-Exempt Status on November 3, 2012, effective January 13, 2012. This charity non-profit tax-deductible status is important for alumni in the US who make large donations.

The Board organized the First TMSAANA General Assembly that was held in Washington, DC, on May 27, 2012. It was well attended by alumni from all over the United States. Ambassador Zewde Retta, a distinguished Ethiopian diplomat, historian and author of *Tafari Makonnen — The Long Journey to Ultimate Power: 1884-1922* and *The Government of Emperor Haile Selasie (1930-1955)*, both in Amharic, was the keynote speaker.

Ambassador Zewde gave a moving address about how the then Crown Prince Tafari Makonnen had a clear vision of the pivotal role of education in leapfrogging Ethiopia into the modern era. During his first long 140-day travels to different European capitals, his consistent request to the governments he visited was not for armaments, as the Ethiopian nobility had wanted him to ask and secure, but for assistance to educate Ethiopia's youth. Unfortunately, his request was not responded to favorably by the European governments. This made him even more determined to establish a modern school using his own funds and by requesting government officials to show their professed "love of country" by donating for the new school.

Ambassador Zewde presented the challenges that the Crown Prince had to overcome in establishing the Tafari Makonnen School. He faced resistance from the traditionalist high officials who were not supportive of the establishment of a secular school that was not run, or at least not strongly supervised, by the Ethiopian Orthodox Church. This was the case of the Menelik II School, the first modern school in Ethiopia established in 1908.

Major Achievements of the First TMSAANA Board

The founding TMSAANA Board laid a strong foundation, which has contributed to the success of TMSAA. Among its notable contributions, were the following:

- Nearly doubled registered alumni members from 118 in August 2011 to 200 in October 2014;

- Launched a TMSAANA website with a photo gallery of TMS teachers and students;

- Began a student support program, based on agreed criteria, that provided financial assistance to 50 needy students for tuition and to help offset costs for monthly hygiene products for girls;

- Provided $3,500 for girls' skills training and capital of $4,600 to start group-organized small businesses in 2012 and 2013;

- Provided 16 desktop computers to the College to expand computer literacy and an advanced sewing machine and other accessories to the textile department;

- Held a meeting in 2013 with the then Addis Ababa mayor and continued the appeal for the restoration of the original TMS name;

- Started an Alumni Visitors Program for knowledge-sharing;

- Initiated an English proficiency course for the College's teachers, which unfortunately did not materialize since the Addis Ababa University (AAU) administration canceled the program it had earlier agreed to provide for the English department.

Second TMSAANA Biennial General Assembly, May 2014 and Second TMSAANA Board of Directors: November 2014 - Oct 2017

As required under the TMSAANA bylaws, the second TMSAANA General Assembly was held two years later, in May 2014, in Washington, DC. Seventy-five alumni, representing 38 percent of TMSAANA members, attended the meeting.

The keynote speaker was the late Ted Vestal, Oklahoma State University Political Science Professor, a former Peace Corps Volunteer (PCV) and later PCV Deputy Director in Ethiopia, and a passionate Ethiopian rights advocate. He addressed the development of modern education in Ethiopia and the significant role played by Tafari Makonnen School in that process. His address was based on his articles on "Modern Education" and "The United States Peace Corps" in Encyclopaedia Aethiopica, a five-volume collection published in Germany. He gave a historical account of education in Ethiopia and the role played by PCVs who taught throughout Ethiopia. Doug Eadie, a key contributor to this book, was among the PCVs who served at TMS between 1964 – 1967.

According to Professor Vestal, under the PCV program, some 1,500 PCVs taught at secondary schools, including at TMS, in 80 locations throughout Ethiopia where they instructed over 300,000 students. The PCVs also taught at Haile Selassie I University, where, in 1965, they accounted for 20% of the University's full-time and part-time faculty. Every year, about 580 PCVs were at work, and 440 were teachers in 58 cities and towns in general secondary, special, and middle schools. His full speech is available on the TMSAA website. It is interesting to note that several TMS alumni who were studying in various graduate schools in the US, some of whom were interviewed by Doug Eadie for this book, had participated in the PCV's training programs at the University of California in Los Angeles (UCLA) or Georgetown University in Washington, D.C., before the PCVs left for their teaching assignments in various parts of Ethiopia.

Recalling President Kennedy's statement that "we will be remembered not for victories or defeats in battle or in politics, but for our contribution to the human spirit," Professor Vestal saluted "TMSAANA's efforts to assist their former school by sharing knowledge, providing financial assistance to needy students, and endeavoring to improve the quality of education are all contributions to the human spirit."

During the Second TMSAANA General Assembly, the Second TMSAANA Board of Directors listed below were elected for a three-year term, November 2014 to October 2017:

1- Bisrat Aklilu, '67 President,

2- Alem Wolde Hawariat, '70, Vice President,

3- Temesgen Petros, '65, Treasurer, (whose term ended in May 2018)

4- Garedew Atnafseged, '68, Secretary,

5- Selam Yisma, '71, Member, and

6- Aklilu Mekonnen, '66, Member (whose term ended in May 2018)

To maintain institutional memory and orderly continuity of the Board, the Board's terms of office are staggered with a three-years term for the President, the Secretary, and the Web Administrator and a two-year term for the Vice President, Treasurer, and other members.

The new Board's initial work plan focused on these priorities:

1) Implementing the decisions of the 2nd TMSAANA General Assembly meeting;

2) Expanding TMSAANA membership and enhancing participation of alumni in TMSAANA activities. Convinced that members are the foundation of any organization, it decided to pursue two specific actions, namely these:

   (a) Identify key alumni contacts by City/Region, and

   (b) Hold Quarterly Regional Meetings by designating TMSAANA Regional Coordinators.

3) Working closely with the Tafari Makonnen School Alumni Charity Association (TMSACA), which was under establishment in Addis Ababa, support the TMS 90th Anniversary Celebration of April 25, 2015, the ongoing effort to restore the TMS name and solidify TMSAANA's support programs to TMS students and teachers.

Establishment of the Addis Ababa-based Tafari Makonnen School Alumni Charity Association (TMSACA): 20 August 2015

In mid-November 2010, during a meeting at TMS, alumni from Ethiopia entered into an agreement with alumnus Petros Aklilu to form an alumni association based in Addis Ababa. However, the process of setting up the alumni association took much longer than expected. Despite the hard work and unrelenting follow up by a small group of dedicated TMS alumni, the process to get approval of the bylaws of the alumni association from the Ethiopian Government's Charities and Societies Agency (CSA), which reviews and gives approval to charity organizations to operate in Ethiopia, was quite long and difficult. CSA required the name of the association to be Tafari Makonnen School Alumni Charity Association (TMSACA) and needed changes in its objectives and organizational structure. It also requested the appointment of a Manager of the Association to which Mrs. Yemesrache Felleke (Class of 1968) was appointed. On 20 August 2015, three years after the first request, TMSACA finally received official legal recognition to work in Ethiopia valid for three years.

The interim TMSACA Founding Committee and the TMSAANA Board agreed to develop and work on a joint TMSACA/TMSAANA 2016/2017 Work Program and Budget for submission to both the TMSACA and TMSAANA General Assemblies. The Work Program focused on supporting an expanded TMSAANA Student Support Program; identification of areas where TMSACA and TMSAANA can provide knowledge-based advisory services to the College, based on the TMS Centennial (2025) Strategic Plan, which was jointly developed by the Entoto College and TMSACA members; promote the publication of books by former TMS teaches and alumni as well as continue to work on the restoration of the TMS name.

The message of the late alumnus, humorist par excellence, and Chairman of TMSACA Board of Directors Getachew Tessema, which he delivered on 18 May 2016 to the Third TMSAANA General Assembly, is contained in Appendix 3. It describes TMSACA's beginnings and difficult journey before it ceased to exist after only one year.

Third TMSAANA Biennial General Assembly, May 2016

The Third TMSAANA General Assembly (GA) took place in Washington, DC, on Sunday, 29 May 2016. A TMS Reunion Dinner preceded the GA on Saturday evening May 28 at Meaza Ethiopian Restaurant in Falls Church, Virginia, which was well attended by alumni, spouses and friends of TMS.

The GA started with a minute of silence in remembrance of alumni who had passed and also Ambassador Zewde Retta, prolific historian, journalist and a great friend of TMS who delivered the First TMSAANA GA keynote address in 2012. I presented a report on the "State of TMSAANA," followed by Board members Selam Yisam on "Membership Development" and Temesgen Petros, TMSAANA treasurer, on "TMSAANA Finances," which are all posted on the TMSAA website under the Third General Assembly tab.

The Board reports were followed by the keynote address, "Remembering Tafari Makonnen," by TMS/TMSAA friend Doug Eadie, a Peace Corps Volunteer at TMS from 1964 to 1967 and currently President & CEO of Doug Eadie & Co. Doug's inspiring and memorable address, reflecting on his years at TMS, was delivered with deep emotions. It is available in its entirety in two videos, on his blog *Entwined Lives* (https://entwinedlives.com) and the TMSAANA website under Third General Assembly.

During the GA, TMSAANA started the practice of giving TMSAANA Awards to Alumni and Friends of TMS under the following two categories:

- *TMS Pioneer Award for Charting the Path for Future TMS Students* is presented to senior alumni. Initially this award recognized membership-dues-paying alumni who attended TMS from 1935 to 1953, but was later extended to include TMSAA members alumni who attended TMS 60 years ago or earlier, i.e., 1964. Under this category more than 50 alumni have received the TMS Pioneer Award.

- *TMS Outstanding Award* or *TMS Award of Gratitude,* presented to TMS alumni (the Founding and First TMSAANA Board of Directors and others) and friends of TMS and/or TMS teachers who have made outstanding contributions to TMSAANA/TMSAA and TMS (Society of Jesus Father Roland Turenne and PCV Doug Eadie, so far).

Table 1: Recipients of "TMS Pioneer Award" in 2016

	Name	Graduation Year	State	Country
1-	Ambassador Imru Zelleke		Virginia	USA
2-	Dr. Aklilu Habte	1950	Maryland	USA
3-	Mr. Yayeherad Fikre	1953	Virginia	USA
5-	Mr. Tesfaye Yemane	1956	Virginia	USA

Table 2: Recipients of the Award of Gratitude for Outstanding Service to TMSAANA in 2016

Name	Function	State	Country
Mr. Petros Aklilu	TMSAANA President 2011-2014	Virginia	USA
Mr. Yirgu Wolde	TMSAANA Board Member 2011-2013	Virginia	USA
Mr. Doug Eadie	TMS PCV Teacher & TMSAANA Friend	Texas	USA
Mr. Ermias Amare	Author of Memoir of a TMS Student	Addis Ababa	Ethiopia
Dr. Moges Gebremariam	TMSAA Champion	Maryland	USA
Mr. Henock Gugsa	TMSAANA Website Administration	Minnesota	USA
Mr. Michael Tesfaye	TMSAANA Website Administration	Virginia	USA

Election of Third Board of Directors

Despite repeated calls for nominations made since the Third TMSAANA General Assembly in May 2016, the Board Nominations and Election Committee (NEC), received no nominations. To broaden the alumni outreach, the Board nominated Dr. Moges Gebremariam, (Washington Area) and Yafet Tekele (Los Angeles area) to join the NEC under the chairmanship of Bayou Tadesse (New York). This however did not achieve a better result since no alumni stepped up for Board membership consideration. As a result, the existing Board members reluctantly agreed to extend their service to May 2018.

Fourth TMSAANA Biennial General Assembly: May 28, 2018

The Fourth biennial General Assembly took place in Washington, DC, on May 28, 2018. The GA received and discussed reports from the TMSAANA President and Treasurer on the activities undertaken by TMSAANA in the previous two years. In addition, a TMSAANA Independent Financial Review was undertaken by

INVITATION TO TMS ALUMNI
4TH TAFARI MAKONNEN SCHOOL ALUMNI ASSOCIATION IN NORTH AMERICA (TMSAANA) BIENNIAL GENERAL ASSEMBLY

Saturday, 26 May 2018 from 10:00 am to 4:00 pm 5700 Columbia Pike, Falls Church, VA. 22041 (Meaza Restaurant)
Information **and** *GA Agenda*

an Independent Financial Professional who issued an unmodified report without any material modifications. These reports are available on the TMSAA website under Fourth General Assembly._

Ato Tekalign Gedamu, Minister of Planning in Emperor Haile Selassie's cabinet and former Vice President of the African Development Bank and author of the book *Republicans on the Throne: A Personal Account of Ethiopia's Modernization and Painful Quest for Democracy* gave an inspiring keynote address in Amharic on "Tafari Makonnen Timhirt Bet: Le Ityopia Yetmhirt Idget Yabereketew Astewatso" ("Tafari Makonnen School's Contribution to Modern Educational Expansion in Ethiopia").

Ato Tekalign highlighted two key areas where TMS made major contribution to education in Ethiopia. The first was through TMS's alumni who went on to occupy major positions in various branches of the Ethiopian government, including the armed forces, and became instrumental in introducing modern methods of administration and management. The second was through the dispatch of senior TMS teachers and graduates to various parts of the country as administrators and teachers. Among the most famous in the second category is the first TMS Director, Dr. (Hakim in Amharic) Workneh Eshete, the first Ethiopian doctor, diplomat and politician, and in the second category, Belata Mersie Hazen Wolde Kirkos, a prominent Amharic and history teacher and later senior government official. They were sent as District Governors to Asbe Teferi and Jigiga districts in Harar province, respectively, to establish modern schools like Tafari Makonnen and introduce modern district administration in these districts. Dr. Workneh requested young TMS alumnus, Emannuel Abraham to join him, which he did. The aim was for other District Governors to emulate them and further expand education and modern district administration, which is what happened.

At the Fourth General Assembly, in addition to reporting TMSAANA's notable achievements in implementing the approved biennial work program, I reported the following two challenges facing TMSAANA, with the second one remaining as a major risk up to now:

1. The limited number of alumni that are TMSAANA members and the inadequacy of membership payments to fund the expanding TMSAANA work program; and

2. The absence of a TMSAANA leadership succession plan poses a major risk for the proper continuity of TMSAANA. This critical issue will be discussed in more detail later.

The Board Nominations Committee chair, alumnus Bayou Tadesse, informed the General Assembly once again that despite repeated calls for Board candidates, no alumnus either volunteered or nominated candidates. As a result, the current Board of Directors, except Mr. Temesgen Petros, who had served for two terms and was unable to continue, were unanimously requested by the General Assembly to serve for another term, until May 2020. In the absence of any alternative, the Board once again reluctantly accepted the request. Subsequent to the General Assembly, the Nominations Committee approached alumna Ms. Merafe Seyoum, who has extensive finance and accounting expertise, to serve as Board Treasurer, which she agreed

Chapter Three: Creation and Growth of the TMSAA

to. The Board, acting on behalf of the General Assembly, conveyed thanks to alumna Merafe and appointed her as Board Treasurer.

The following is the list of the Third TMSAANA Board of Directors:

1- **Bisrat Aklilu, '67, President,**

2- **Alem W. Hawariat '70, Vice President,**

3- **Garedew Atnafseged,'68, Secretary,**

4- **Merafe Seyoum,'68, Treasurer, and**

5- **Selam Yisma '71, Member**

During the Fourth General Assembly, the following alumni and Friends of TMS received TMS Pioneer and Gratitude awards.

Table 3: Recipients of the "TMS Pioneer Award" in 2018				
	Name	Grad Year	State/Region	Country
1	The late Fitawrari Makonnen Dori	1956	Kentucky	USA
2	The late Captain Demissie Negusie	1958	Washington, DC	USA
3	Major Argaw Kabtamu	1958	Addis Ababa	Ethiopia
4	Eng. Berhanu Woldamlak	1960	Addis Ababa	Ethiopia
5	Mr. Abera Abdi	1960	Maryland	USA
6	The late Mr. Fekade Bizuneh	1960	Georgia	USA

Table 4: Recipients of Awards of Gratitude for Outstanding Service to TMSAANA in 2018

	Name	Function	State	Country
1	The late Ms. Tsehay Elias	TMSAANA Treasurer 2011-2012	Virginia	USA
2	Mr. Temesgen Petros	TMSAANA Treasurer 2013-2108	Virginia	USA
3	Mr. Mack Mesfin Mekasha	TMSAANA Website Administrator	Virginia	USA
4	Mr. Hoyt Smith	TMS Peace Corps Volunteer 1965-68	Texas	USA
5	Ms. Abebayehu Gebremariam	Benefactor	Maryland	USA
6	The late Mr. Solomon Bekele	Benefactor	Maryland	USA
7	Mr. Tekalign Gedamu	2018 GA Keynote Speaker	Pennsylvania	USA

Fifth TMSAANA Biennial General Assembly of May 2020

The Board had started preparation to hold the Fifth TMSAANA General Assembly in Washington, DC, during the May 2020 Memorial weekend when the COVID-19 pandemic that paralyzed the world struck. The COVID-19 lockdown led to the cancellation of the meeting. The Fifth General Assembly was an important event since four of the six Board members who had served six or more years since October 2014 were due to hand over their Board responsibilities to new Board members. The COVID-19 lockdown unfortunately forced the Board to again continue its service until the next biannual General Assembly of May 2022.

Name Change of TMSAANA to Tafari Makonnen School Alumni Association (TMSAA)

While in Addis Ababa in September 2021, I visited the Ethiopian Agency for Civil Society Organization (ACSO), previously known as Charities and Societies Agency (CSA), to inquire about the status of registration of TMSACA. I was informed that TMSACA's 2015 registration license has been revoked for over two years due to noncompliance of reporting and reregistration requirements. I convened a meeting with TMSACA members, along with TMSAANA members who were in Addis, and proposed we take advantage of the registration cancellation to unify the TMS alumni association worldwide by amending the TMSAANA Bylaws instead of seeking to reregister TMSACA as a separate association. The Director General of ACSO had confirmed to me that TMSAANA, as a foreign NGO, can be registered by ACSO with a representative office in Addis Ababa if it has legitimate operations in Ethiopia, gets a letter of recommendation from the Ethiopian Embassy in Washington, DC, and fulfills other ACSO requirements.

On 15 April 2022, the TMSAANA Board held a meeting with the TMSAANA Founding Board and reviewed the amended TMSAANA Bylaw, changing TMSAANA to TMSAA and some of the Bylaw provisions to make it a unified global organization. The joint Board unanimously approved the changes and decided to send it to the TMSAANA General Assembly. The changes to the revised TMSAA Bylaw were highlighted and following Article VII Section 1 of the TMSAANA Bylaw, alumni were informed that the Bylaw can be altered or amended by a simple majority vote of regular members constituting the TMSAANA General Assembly.

As a result, alumni were requested to send by 15 April 2022 their approval or non-approval of the joint Board's decision to change TMSAANA to TMSAA, as of 14 October 2021. Since the amendment was unanimously approved, the Tafari Makonnen School Alumni Association in North America (TMSAANA) was changed to Tafari Makonnen School Alumni Association (TMSAA), retroactive effective as of 14 October 2021.

Membership to TMSAA was made open to the worldwide alumni of TMS and its successors (Entoto Comprehensive Academic and Vocational School (ECAVS), Entoto Technical and Vocational Training College (ETVTC) and Entoto Polytechnic College (EPTC). A new Certificate of Registration as TMSAA was also requested from the District of Columbia government. The decision to re-establish the association as TMSAA, unifying the worldwide TMS alumni under one organization, was warmly welcomed by TMSAANA members, particularly those residing in Europe and Africa. In the past they had rightly complained that as full-fledged dues-paying members they were being treated as "stepchildren" by naming only "North America" in the Alumni Association name.

The new TMSAA Bylaw calls for up to nine Board of Directors, taking into consideration the need for representation from North America, Ethiopia and other continents where TMSAA members reside. The Board conducted consultation with alumni and invited the following four Addis Ababa-based TMS alumni to join the new nine-member TMSAA Board:

1   Artist Debebe Eshetu 1957;
2   Captain Kebede Woldestadik 1970;
4   Mrs. Tsigereda Tafesse 1995; and
5   Artist Lulseged Retta 1970.

Mrs. Tsigereda Tafesse was appointed as Board Secretary and also as TMSAA Ethiopia Representative, the latter as per the requirement of the Ethiopian Agency for Civil Society Organization. The revised TMSAA Bylaws as well as other TMSAA Legal Documents are posted in the TMSAA website under About Us/Legal Documents.

The new Board subsequently arranged to hold the First TMSAA Global General Assembly Zoom meeting in May 2022 to report on TMSAA activities being implemented jointly with the TMS/Entoto Polytechnic College and facilitate the first virtual face to face meeting of alumni after the COVID-19 lockdown.

The First TMSAA Global General Assembly Zoom Meeting: 4 June 2022

The First TMSAA Global General Assembly Zoom meeting took place on 4 June 2022. As this was the first TMS alumni global meeting, the Board worked hard to make it interesting, informative and forward-looking. The meeting was designed to not only inspire TMS alumni, but also to motivate alumni of other Ethiopian schools to support their alma maters and help ensure that current students at their schools receive the quality education and life-changing opportunities alumni were privileged to have received.

The Global General Assembly brought together for the first time alumni residing in Ethiopia, Africa, Canada, Europe and USA. It was addressed by distinguished alumni and TMS teachers including the late Ambassador Imiru Zelleke, who was then ninety-nine years old. Other major speakers included TMS 1960 graduate and third President of Addis Ababa University Dr. Aklilu Habte; the late Mr. (as he was called at TMS) Roland Turenne, who was 98 years old and was the only Canadian Jesuit TMS teacher alive at that time; and Mr. Doug Eadie, a 1964-67 Peace Corps Volunteer and key contributor of this book. In addition, the then EPTC Dean, Teshome Feissa, who worked closely with the TMSAA Board for the restoration of the TMS name and many TMS and Entoto Comprehensive Academic and Vocational School (ECAVS) and Entoto Technical and Vocational Training College (ETVTC) alumni addressed the meeting.

During the Assembly, noting the 2021 extremely low percentage of alumni paying the $120 annual membership payment, 14% or 31 out of 214 alumni members, alumnus Tesfaye Aklilu (Class of 1964) proposed an "alumni challenge" to double the membership payment by end 2022. While alumni responded to the "alumni challenge" by increasing the payment to 24%, (51 out of 214), it fell short of the agreed-upon doubling target. As the membership payment issue is critical to the proper continuation of TMSAA, it is discussed later in more detail.

To better illustrate the wide-ranging scope and participation of the First Global General Assembly meeting, I have included its full agenda in Appendix I.

TMSAA Chapters/TMS Centennial Committees Establishment

As TMSAA is a fully and totally voluntary alumni-led-and managed organization, the full range of its tasks, from contacting alumni, managing the contributions, formulating the assistance program in close partnership with the TMS/Entoto Polytechnic College and monitoring and reporting the funded activities, is undertaken by the TMSAA Board of Directors, with the President in the lead role. With the global expansion of TMSAA, compared to the North America focus of TMSAANA, the proper execution of these tasks became increasingly difficult. As a result, I proposed to the Board the establishment of more formal TMSAA Chapters, compared to the earlier informal regional TMSAA networks. The Board agreed the establishment of TMSAA Chapters is not only timely but will also promote the active participation of TMS alumni in the planning and implementation of the coming historic TMS Centennial of 27 April 2025.

In this regard, the TMSAA Board made the following two decisions:

1. Requested the College Dean (at that time, Mr. Teshome Feissa) to prepare a "TMS Centennial Celebration Document," which he did superbly. The document was later reviewed and endorsed by the Board.

2. Decided on formal establishment of TMS Chapters and TMS Centennial Committees (TMSCC) in different geographic areas globally where TMS alumni live. The TMSCCs responsibility is to review and discuss the TMS Centennial Celebration Document and Centennial activities with their respective Chapter members, as well as with TMSCCs of other Chapters, and provide comments and suggestions to the Board, including proposing possible TMS Centennial projects for funding consideration.

Using the TMSAA alumni database, which though incomplete provides essential info on alumni, and my knowledge of and contacts with the active TMS alumni in the different countries, regions and states, I engaged with the active alumni which led to the establishment of eleven TMSAA Chapters and TMS Centennial Committees (TMSCC), shown in Table 5. To assist the TMSCCs, I had a TMS Centennial tab created on the TMSAA website, with sub-pages for each TMSAA Chapter TMSCC, displaying their members with their photos.

The eleven TMSCCs met with the TMSAA Board on 30 March 2024 and endorsed to fund as a Centennial project, an Arts-cum-Academic multi-purpose "TMSAA Building."

The TMSCCs confirmed their commitment to:

1. Increase their 2024 Chapter membership fee payment rate to a minimum of 75%, and

2. Explore various ways of fundraising for the Centennial TMSAA Building, including requesting special donations from their Chapter members, Friends of TMS, private and public organizations.

Table 5: TMSAA Chapters and TMS Centennial Committees (TMSCC)	
1) Canada TMSCC	**7) Georgia, USA, TMSCC**
1) Mr. Fikre Mariam Tsehay	1) Mr. Moges Alemu
2) Mr. Assefa Kebede	2) Late Mr. Fekadeseleasssie Bizuneh
3) Mr. Dawit Beyene	3) Mr. Teferl Chernet
2) Ethiopia TMSCC	**8) Mid-West MI/MN/OH/WI/ TMSCC**
1) Major Argaw Kabtamu	1) Mr. Zewdie Hailu, Minnesota
2) Mrs. Tsigereda Tafesse	2) Mrs. Wegayehu Asefa, Michigan
3) Mrs. Yemesrache Felleke	3) Mr. Assefa Damte, Wisconsin
4) Mr. Solomon Teshome Retta	4) Dr. Ermias Seleshi, Ohio
5) Mrs. Azeb Asrat	5) Dr. Mesfin Tadesse, Ohio
6) Mrs. Martha Habtemariam Massa	6) Mr. Girma Felleke, Ohio
7) Mrs. Asrat Tilahun	
8) Ms. Ayehuberhan Lemma	

Table 5: TMSAA Chapters and TMS Centennial Committees (TMSCC)

3) Europe TMSCC
1) Dr. Fantu Cheru, Sweden
2) Mr. Dejene Tezera, Austria
3) Mr. Fekade Zewde, UK
4) Dr. Abebe Zegeye, UK
5) Dr. Shewangizaw Teshome, Germany
6) Ms. Suzi Lemma, Germany

4) Middle East TMSCC
1) Mr. Busera Awel, UAE
2) Mr. Girma Abate, UAE
3) Mr. Ibrahim Zekeria, Saudi Arabia

5) Southern Africa TMSCC
1) Dr. Mohammad Kamil Sherif, Botswana
2) Mr. Fisseha Tsion Tekie, South Africa

6) DMV, USA, TMSCC
1) Mrs. Meaza Bekele Wegayheu
2) Dr. Moges Gebremariam
3) Mr. Getachew Tesfaye
4) Mrs. Selamawit Getachew
5) Ms. Yeshiareg Dejene
6) Mr. Tadesse Goshime
7) Ms. Seble Mekonnen
8) Mr. Tesfu Zegeye

9) Tetra-State Conn/NJ/NY/Mass TMSCC
1) Mr. Petros Aklilu, New Jersey
2) Mr. Yirgu Wolde, New Jersey
3) Mrs. Berhan Eshete, New York
4) Dr. Wondwessen Bekele, New Jersey
5) Mr. Yonathan Fassil, Massachusetts

10) South California TMSCC
1) Mr. Meheretu Belete
2) Ms. Berhane Tesfaye
3) Mr. Daniel Yohannes
4) Prof. Meskerem Tadesse
5) Mr. Gardew Lemma

11) Texas TMSCC
1) Mr. Abate Kebede
2) Mrs. Tarik Teferi Sunega
3) Mr. Tedla Zewde
4) Ms. Almaz Woldeab

Second Global General Assembly Zoom Meeting: 29 June 2024

As the TMS Centennial of 27 April 2025 was approaching, the TMSAA Second Global General Assembly meeting focused on the TMS Centennial activities being planned, in close partnership with the EPTC.

As the previous Dean of TMS/EPTC, Mr. Teshome Feissa, underscored in presenting the planned TMS Centennial Celebration, very few are as fortunate to celebrate a Centennial as TMS alumni are. He expressed his hope and expectation that before the Centennial Celebration, the TMS name will be restored, the TMS gate with its restored name will be constructed and the foundations of the "TMSAA Building" will be laid. He also informed alumni that the ISO certification of the College is well underway. He emphasized how the close and seamless relationship between the College and TMSAA is an ideal model for a school-alumni relationship.

The General Assembly provided an opportunity for alumni to hear from the 11 Chapter TMSCCs about their plans and suggestions for the TMS Centennial. The Chapters, while successful in mobilizing additional TMS alumni because of the Centennial, highlighted the large pool of TMS alumni who still have to be mobilized to join TMSAA.

The agenda of the Second Global General Assembly meeting is presented in Appendix II. During the General Assembly, the following alumni, who graduated 60 years ago (1964) or earlier and are TMSAA members, were presented with a TMS Pioneer Award.

Table 6: Recipients of the TMS Pioneer Award in 2024

	Name	Grad Year	State/Region	Country
1	Mr. Seyoum Alemayheu	1952	Addis Ababa	Ethiopia
2	Mr. Mohamed Ibrahim	1953	California	USA
3	Mr. Tedla Teshome	1954	Addis Ababa	Ethiopia
4	Mr. Addis Anteneh Kassa	1955	Addis Ababa	Ethiopia

	Name	Grad Year	State/Region	Country
	Table 6: Recipients of the TMS Pioneer Award in 2024			
5	Major Hailemariam Abai	1955	Maryland	USA
6	Mr. Mealk Tefera	1955	Addis Ababa	Ethiopia
7	Mr. Mengesha Workneh	1955	Addis Ababa	Ethiopia
8	Mr. Ephrem Kebede	1958	Paris	France
9	Mr. Telahun Workeneh Eshetu	1959	Addis Ababa	Ethiopia
10	Mr. Taye-Brook Zerihoun	1959	New Jersey	USA
11	Mr. Abebe Tefera	1960	New Mexico	USA
12	Eng. Berhanu Woldamlak	1960	Addis Ababa	Ethiopia
13	Mr. Fisseh Tsion Tekie	1960	Johannesburg	South Africa
14	Dr. Ayele Mekuria	1960	Addis Ababa	Ethiopia
15	Dr. Mekonnen Tefera	1960	Addis Ababa	Ethiopia
16	Colonel Tsegaye Wanna	1960	Addis Ababa	Ethiopia
17	Mr. Moges Ayalew	1960	Addis Ababa	Ethiopia
18	Mr.Yilma Seyoum Mafegn	1960	Addis Ababa	Ethiopia
19	Mr. Shewangizaw Agonafir	1961	California	Ethiopia
20	Dr. Dawit Zewde	1962	Addis Ababa	Ethiopia
21	Mr. Daniel Jote Mesfin	1962	Addis Ababa	Ethiopia

Table 6: Recipients of the TMS Pioneer Award in 2024

	Name	Grad Year	State/Region	Country
22	Eng. Eskinder Zewde	1962	Berlin	Germany
23	Mr. Fassil Gabremariam	1962	Florida	USA
24	Dr. Tesfaye Aklilu	1962	Connecticut	USA
25	Mr. Yilma Kassaye	1962	Virginia	USA
26	Mr. Wondem Teferra	1963	Delaware	USA

Table 7: Recipients of Award of Gratitude for Outstanding Service to TMSAANA in 2024

	Name	Function	Region/State	Country
1	Mr. Tafesse Bogale	President of TMS 75th Anniversary Committee	Addis Ababa	Ethiopia
2	Dean Teshome Feissa	Ex-Dean of EPTC/TMS	Addis Ababa	Ethiopia

Restoration of the TMS Name

As reported in the various Board Updates, TMSAA has continuously followed up with the Addis Ababa City Administration (AACA) regarding our long-standing request since the year 2000, during the 75th Anniversary of TMS, for the restoration of the TMS name. Between the TMSAANA Founding Board of 2011-2014 and the current Board, our TMS name restoration request has been submitted to four Addis Ababa city mayors. We were asked to provide many official written justifications for the name change to various Federal and Addis Ababa City Bureaus, which we did. All the mayors informed us the request is justified but the name change needs to follow the legal procedures for such a change.

In 2020, teachers and students of the College unanimously voted and submitted a signed request to the AACA for the restoration of the TMS name. Mrs. Adanech Abebe, the current Mayor of Addis Ababa, clearly informed Artist Debebe Eshetu, during a meeting he had with her in her office on this subject, that the TMS name restoration will be done, which was indeed done in February 2025.

TMSAA Website

The TMSAA website has the best features of a good website. It is easy to navigate with the menu items easily accessible from any page. It is web-friendly, visually attractive and has substantive information. Alumni are regularly recommended to visit the website since it provides a wealth of info on TMS and TMSAA, including notices on major TMS and TMSAA activities. The TMS Centennial is displayed with a time counter showing the months, days and seconds to the Centennial date of 27 April 2025. The Photo and Video Galleries contain memorable photos and videos of TMS, TMSAA activities, It contains photos of TMS teachers, alumni group photos, and recently TMS Scouts. Alumni who have class and/or group photos from their TMS days are regularly requested to send them for posting on the Photo Gallery.

TMSAA WhatsApp Group

The TMSAA WhatsApp Group has become the primary channel of communications and exchange among alumni and continues to be lively and informative. The TMSAA WhatsApp Group Code of Conduct requires alumni to only post about TMS and TMSAA issues. Postings of a political or religious nature or of no relevance to TMS/TMSAA readers are removed by the WhatsApp administrators. To date more than 350 alumni have joined the TMSAA WhatsApp Group and alumni who have not yet joined are encouraged to join by contacting any Board member.

TMS Alumni by Country, Region and TMS Graduating Year

TMSAA alumni, as indeed members of any Ethiopian global alumni association, are interested to know where their schoolmates are today and if they are members of their alumni associations. This is because in the 1970s, Ethiopians began moving to different countries of the world, forced by the brutal conditions imposed by the miliary dictatorship.

To respond to this interest, I regularly send requests to alumni through the TMSAA WhatsApp and the periodic Board Updates to fill out the TMSAA Member Contact Form. Unfortunately, not all alumni fill out the form making the data incomplete. The data from the TMSAA Member Contact form (https://shorturl.at/CwNZs) is also used by the various TMSAA Chapters in the planning of periodic TMSAA activities and get-togethers.

The results of the data gathered are given on page 148.

TMSAA Membership Distribution

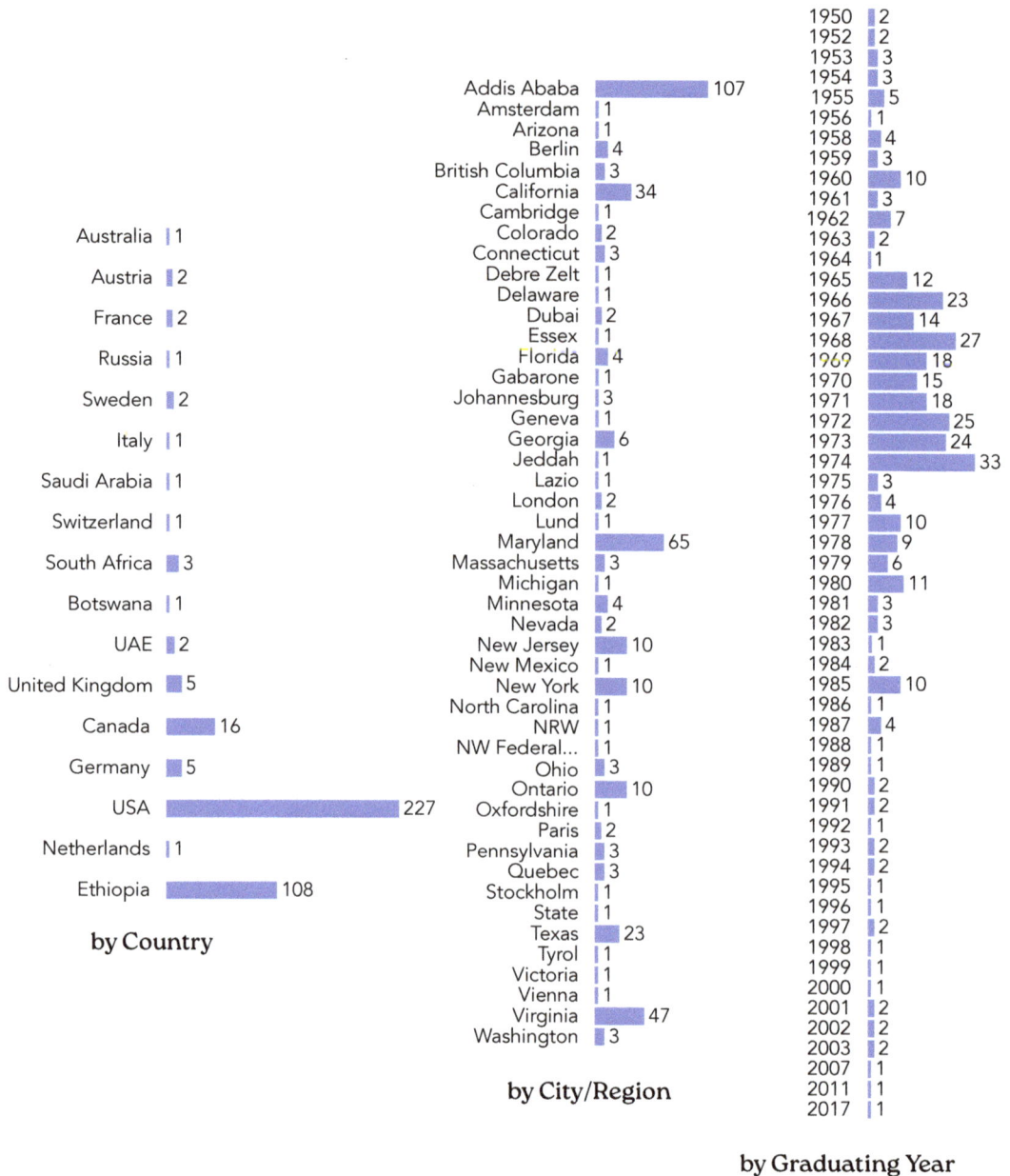

by Country

Country	Count
Australia	1
Austria	2
France	2
Russia	1
Sweden	2
Italy	1
Saudi Arabia	1
Switzerland	1
South Africa	3
Botswana	1
UAE	2
United Kingdom	5
Canada	16
Germany	5
USA	227
Netherlands	1
Ethiopia	108

by City/Region

City/Region	Count
Addis Ababa	107
Amsterdam	1
Arizona	1
Berlin	4
British Columbia	3
California	34
Cambridge	1
Colorado	2
Connecticut	3
Debre Zelt	1
Delaware	1
Dubai	2
Essex	1
Florida	4
Gabarone	1
Johannesburg	3
Geneva	1
Georgia	6
Jeddah	1
Lazio	1
London	2
Lund	1
Maryland	65
Massachusetts	3
Michigan	1
Minnesota	4
Nevada	2
New Jersey	10
New Mexico	1
New York	10
North Carolina	1
NRW	1
NW Federal...	1
Ohio	3
Ontario	10
Oxfordshire	1
Paris	2
Pennsylvania	3
Quebec	3
Stockholm	1
State	1
Texas	23
Tyrol	1
Victoria	1
Vienna	1
Virginia	47
Washington	3

by Graduating Year

Year	Count
1950	2
1952	2
1953	3
1954	3
1955	5
1956	1
1958	4
1959	3
1960	10
1961	3
1962	7
1963	2
1964	1
1965	12
1966	23
1967	14
1968	27
1969	18
1970	15
1971	18
1972	25
1973	24
1974	33
1975	3
1976	4
1977	10
1978	9
1979	6
1980	11
1981	3
1982	3
1983	1
1984	2
1985	10
1986	1
1987	4
1988	1
1989	1
1990	2
1991	2
1992	1
1993	2
1994	2
1995	1
1996	1
1997	2
1998	1
1999	1
2000	1
2001	2
2002	2
2003	2
2007	1
2011	1
2017	1

Annual Membership Payments

A major challenge facing TMSAA since TMSAANA's establishment in 2011 is the lack of consistent member support through regular membership payments. Membership payment forms the bedrock of any organization's survival and financial health, ensuring the agreed programs of support are funded. TMSAA has made major improvements in its membership collection system making it easy for members to make payments through many payment methods — check, online credit or debit card, bank transfer, telephone transfer/ Zelle.

	Table 8: Annual Membership Payment 2011-2025		
Year	Registered Alumni	Paying Alumni	% Paying Alumni
2011	138	48	35
2012	180	64	36
2013	200	51	26
2014	200	42	21
2015	213	62	29
2016	213	32	15
2017	214	58	27
2018	214	44	21
2019	214	23	11
2020	214	35	16
2021	214	31	14
2022	214	51	24
2023	214	88	41
2024	350	233	68
As of 31/3/2025	480	105	22

Nevertheless, as seen from Table 8, until 2023 TMSAA membership payments continued to be inadequate, with less than 30 percent alumni paying the agreed annual payment ($120 for alumni outside Ethiopia and ETB 1,200 for alumni in Ethiopia). Thankfully, several alumni began paying multiyear membership payments ranging from two to fifteen years, while some alumni made additional general purpose unearmarked donations.

The 2023 membership payment of 41%, while higher than 2022, is still unsatisfactorily low for an alumni organization. At the February 2024 Board meeting, I presented two options for 2024 membership payment — a target of 50% or a more ambitious target of 75% of the 350 registered alumni. The Board agreed on the ambitious target of 75%. Since the TMSAA Chapters were requested to reach out to their Chapter members, I set up an ongoing membership payment-monitoring report (Table 9) and share it regularly with Chapters and alumni.

Table 9: 2024 Membership Payment by TMSAA Chapters

	TMSAA Chapters As of 20 Dec 2024,	No of Registered[3] Alumni Members	2024 Alumni Membership Payment	
		No	No	%
1	Canada	15	10	67
2	Ethiopia	89	78	88
3	Europe	19	12	63
4	Southern Africa	4	4	100
5	Middle East	3	3	100

3 The number of "Registered members" in TMSAA is difficult to clearly define since alumni do not need to register to participate in TMSAA The number reflects alumni who receive regular TMSAA information. Due to the TMS Centennial, it has recently increased and will at least reach 500 in 2025.

Table 9: 2024 Membership Payment by TMSAA Chapters

	TMSAA Chapters As of 20 Dec 2024,	No of Registered[3] Alumni Members	2024 Alumni Membership Payment	
		No	No	%
6	DMV (DC/MD/VA)	105	43	41
7	Georgia	6	4	66
8	Tetra-State Conn/Mass/NJ/NY	21	21	100
9	Midwest (MI/MN/WI)	5	3	60
10	North California	10	8	80
11	Ohio	3	3	100
12	South California	26	21	81
13	Texas	19	14	74
14	Alumni in Chapter Countries/Locations	325	224	69
15	Alumni in non-Chapter Countries/Locations	25	9	36
16	Grand Total	350	233	67
17	TMSAA Board Target -75% of registered Alumni	262	233	90
White: Payments above the 75% target. Orange: payments under the Board Target of 75%.				

TMS/EPTC and TMSAA Memorandum of Understanding

The TMS/EPTC and TMSAA Memorandum of Understanding (MOU) was signed on 6 March 2024 and sets up a comprehensive institutional collaboration and partnership between the two aimed at assisting EPTC to regain TMS's earlier reputation. The partnership will strengthen the current knowledge sharing, material support, and advice that TMSAA is providing EPTC. As indicated in the MOU, "achieving the goals of the partnership requires imagination, teamwork, and commitment using shared resources"

TMSAA Support to TMS/ EPTC
Expanded TMSAA Student Support Program

The oldest and most important TMSAA program designed to support TMS/Entoto Polytechnic is the student support program. It was started by the Founding Board under TMSAANA and includes two types of support to students who are vetted by the College:

1. A merit- and needs-based Tuition Payment program for both male and female students. Selection criteria include the student's satisfactory class performance and family income determined to be insufficient to support the student.

2. A purely needs-based support for female students to cover monthly costs for sanitary pads.

This program expanded 16-fold from 50 students in 2014 to a peak of 800 in 2017, due largely to increasing support for female students. It is not the annual alumni membership payment that enabled TMSAA to provide this expanded support to students but rather the generous special contributions of some alumni. Special mention must be made of alumnus Dr. Moges Gebremariam (Class of 1965) who year after year donated generously to this program by mobilizing his immediate family, friends and his officemates to provide TMSAA with additional funding.

During the COVID -19 years of 2020 to 2022, the repeated closure of schools and the college administration's decision to reassess the eligibility of students for TMSAA support led to a scaling down of the TMSAA support program. TMSAA continued to provide the monthly sanitary supplies support to female students even during the COVID -19 closure of the College. In recent years, to ensure proper accountability, it was decided to make support payments directly to bank accounts of eligible students and stop cash payment. While the College partnered with banks to come to the campus and help students open bank accounts, many students were not willing to open bank accounts thereby forfeiting the support program.

Computer Training and Related Assistance

In 2012, the First TMSAANA Board supplied 16 desktop computers to the College IT Department to establish a computer training program for students. The training was so popular that each student was limited to only one-hour computer use. In addition, one teaching Sewing Machine was delivered to the Apparel Department and one tricycle was purchased for a disabled student who was travelling a long distance to the College using a hand-powered tricycle.

Because of the popularity of computer training classes, the College's requested that TMSAA fund a separate computer training class for female and disabled students. The first TMSAANA computer training class was dominated by male students and without this added funding, female students would be unable to get access. To rectify this, TMSAANA provided a second computer training class exclusively for female students with seven desktop computers, one printer, and one scanner.

Restoration of TMS Water Fountain

With the unreserved support of engineer Berhanu Woldamalak (class of 1960), TMSAANA restored our memorable TMS water fountain that was built more than 90 years ago. The water fountain is another iconic artifact that evokes fond

Restored Stone Water Fountain

memories among many TMS alumni. Over the years, it fell into disrepair for lack of maintenance, and it was restored meticulously by engineer Berhanu to its original form, using improved water pipes and the same type of stone that was originally used when it was built. It was inaugurated on 8 December 2016 in the presence of the Dean, teachers and students of the College, TMSACA and TMSAANA Board members and alumni. As shown on page 153, a plaque is prominently displayed on the fountain explaining its restoration by TMSACA and TMSAANA. Pictures of the inauguration event are posted on the TMSAANA website at Photo Gallery/Water Fountain Restoration Inauguration.

TMSAA Office at TMS/EPTC

TMSAA is grateful to Dean Semeneh Abesha, the College Dean in early 2022, for taking final action on TMSAANA/TMSAA's continuous requests for an alumni office at the College that would facilitate regular and smooth coordination with the College. The TMSAA Office is in the main TMS "Church" building in the room that used to be the TMS Bank under the supervision of Mr. Marcel Gareau. A group of alumni participated in the Alumni Office acceptance event and funded the renovation and equipping of the Office, along with landscaping and painting of the center court in front of the Alumni Office[4]. The office was furnished with in-kind donations of alumni.

Mr. Yitayew Neguisse, College Trainer and graduate of the College, is the TMSAA liaison. He is available at the Alumni Office and can be reached at +251 910 012 259.

---

4 ETB 50,000 each by Captain Kebede Woldetsadik, Tesfaye Aklilu, Petros Aklilu, Alem W/Mathias, Garedew Atnafseged and Bisrat Aklilu and ETB 10,000 by Tsigereda Tafesse. In addition, alumna Yemserach Felleke gave an old large photo of Ras Tafari Makonnen that is on the wall of the alumni office, while an alumni group, Yirgu Wolde, Brook Bekele, Solomon Worde Kal and Israel Tekele, provided the Office desk.

TMSAA Food Sharing/Blessing Event

TMSAA, and previously TMSAANA, has been hosting two Food Sharing/Blessing events during the year on the occasions of the Ethiopian New Year and Easter/Eid Al-Fitr. The program is funded through a special Food Sharing donation voluntarily provided by alumni. Working in partnership with the College, these Food Sharing offerings are given to families from the College, and families living near the College, earning income judged to be inadequate to support their basic food needs. Typically, they are provided a food basket of chicken, eggs, wheat flour, macaroni/pasta and cooking oil.

One of the Food Sharing/Blessing Events

The food basket composition and quantity depend on the success of the Board's fund mobilization. When the voluntarily mobilized funds are inadequate to fund the minimum food basket for the eligible families, the Board allocates the required balance from TMSAA general funds. A special Food Sharing Donation tab was created on the TMSAA website (under "Donate Now" and "Donation Type") to collect ongoing donations from interested alumni for future events. Alumni in Ethiopia also make similar donations through the TMSAA Addis Awash Bank.

The COVID-19 years of 2020-2023, which led to drastic scaling down of economic activities, inflicted major hardship on the low-income families both at the College and within its vicinity. Most lost their limited earnings and were unable to meet the basic food needs of their families. The TMSAA Board members responded with special voluntary contributions and requested alumni to join. Several alumni eagerly responded as appeals for special donations was already established under the biannual Food Sharing program. Videos and Photos of the distribution of these donations, including testimony of recipients, are posted on the TMSAA website Photo Gallery and Video Gallery; see TMSAANA ውስታ _መላሾች _Fighting COVID-19 Third Food Donation.

TMSAA Support to Those Affected by Drought in Borena and to the Displaced in Debre Berhan

As Ethiopian citizens or citizens of Ethiopian origin, despite TMSAA's limited financial resources, TMS alumni have readily responded when called to do so to assist Ethiopians in crisis. This was the case in early 2023 when the then Dean of the College, Mr. Teshome Feissa, requested alumni to assist our sisters and brothers in Borena suffering from drought, as well as citizens forcefully displaced by conflicts in their places of origin, and forced to move to camps in Debre Berhan.

The appeal for Borena was finalized in a week and received 300,000 ETB, while the subsequent Debre Berhan appeal received 800,000 ETB for a total of 1.1 million ETB. TMSAA is grateful to 65 alumni who generously donated. Special thanks is again due to alumnus Dr. Moges Gebremariam, who initially donated 200,000 ETB by mobilizing his family and friends, and subsequently challenged alumni with a matching donation of 120,000 ETB, resulting in an additional 240,000 ETB.

In line with TMSAA's status as a 501(c)(3) nonprofit and charity organization in the USA, the Board procured emergency food and animal feed (two truckloads) and dispatched it to Borena, along with similar donations from Entoto Polytechnic College and other Polytechnic Colleges in Addis Ababa.

Displaced Children in Debre Berhan Receiving TMSAA Support

For the Debre Berhan campaign, the Board sent an assessment team comprising Board members, the Dean, and staff of the College to see firsthand the situation of the displaced and discuss with humanitarian coordinators on the ground the best ways to utilize the mobilized TMSAA funds. The team visited Debre Berhan in March 2023 and proposed to the Board the provision of wheat flour, blankets, and emergency food for children to the newly arrived displaced individuals in two separate camps (China and Woinshet) who did not receive any support from other organizations. Wheat flour (4,000 kgs), energy food (1,104 kg Fafa) for over 1,000 children and blankets for 475 families were directly bought by TMSAA and delivered in two batches to the displaced.

TMSAA Support for the Publication of Books about TMS:

As I Remember Them...Memoirs of a former TMS teacher by Roland Turenne, SJ. Mr. Turenne, as he was known at TMS, was the last of the Canadian Jesuit group that taught at TMS starting in 1945. He passed away in Quebec, Canada, on December 9, 2023, just short of two months before his 100th birthday on Valentine's Day, February 14, 1924. Mr. Turenne spent 60 years in Ethiopia, first at TMS for 17 years (1957-1974), teaching geography until the military dictatorship (Derg) that overthrew the Emperor and changed TMS's name forced the Canadian Jesuits and other foreign TMS teachers to leave. He spent the next 43 years until 2017 serving in various parts of Ethiopia as a geography teacher at Debre Zeit; a social worker with French NGOs in Afar, Gemu Gofa, and Kaffa; Head of the Ethiopian Jesuit Relief Service; Chaplain in Waliso; and Administrator and later a retiree resident at the Galilee Center in Bishoftu.

In *As I Remember Them. . . . Memoirs of a Former TMS Teacher,* **Mr.** Turenne wrote about his Jesuit brothers who taught at TMS. TMSAA published the book in 2016.

Mr. Turenne donated his work and the book's copyright to TMSAANA, writing in his introduction, "I offer these pages most especially to the former students of TMS residing both in Ethiopia as well as dispersed in many foreign countries around the world. Like migrant birds, TMS alumni always return to their native Ethiopia and their beloved TMS to rem-iniscence about the 'good old days' in their old TMS. ...I am grateful to the Tafari Makonnen School Alumni Association in North America (TMSAANA) for financing the publication of my book."

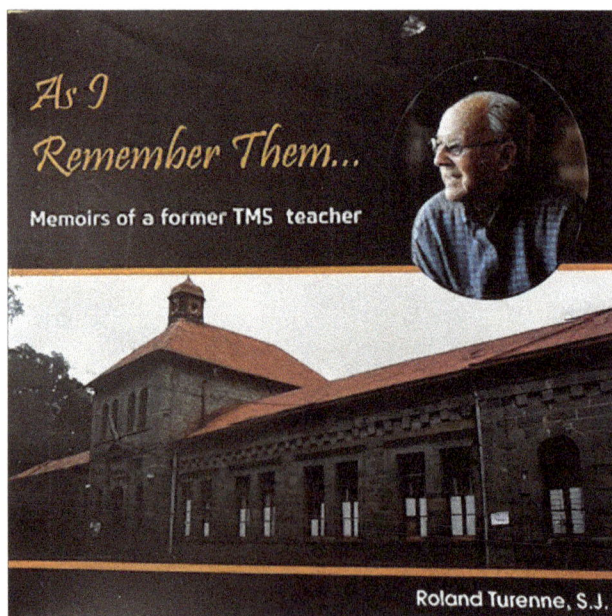

As I Remember Them...
Memoirs of a former TMS teacher
Roland Turenne, S.J.

In July 2016, alumni Berhanu Woldeamlak, the late Minas Lessanu, Sahlu Haile and I visited him at his resi-dence in Bishoftu. We were pleased to present him with the

TMS Gratitude Award he received at the TMSAANA May 2016 General Assembly "For writing his TMS memoir and his lifelong service to TMS and Ethiopia." During our meeting, he passionately expressed his wish to be buried in Ethiopia, stating he had no desire to leave, even for medical reasons, as his TMS teaching colleague Mr. Gerald Gagnon had chosen to do. Mr. Gagnon elected to go to Nairobi for medical care where he died and was buried in a country he did not work in, or know, like Ethiopia. Mr. Turenne repeatedly told us that we should be witnesses to his wish.

Mr. Turenne Proudly Displays His TMS Gratitude Award, 2016

Sadly, in 2017, he was ordered by the Jesuit Provincial Superior to either move to an infirmary in Kenya or return to Canada out of concern for his health. He left Ethiopia with great reluctance for a Jesuit retirement center in Quebec, Canada. When alumni Dr. Moges Gebremariam, Bayou Tadesse, my wife, Delawit, and I visited him in 2018, he was so overjoyed that, for the first time, he agreed to leave his residence and dine at a restaurant in the city were where he continuously and proudly announced to the people dining that we were his students from Ethiopia!

Since he made me promise to visit him again, my wife and I traveled to Quebec and visited him in 2021, 2022, and, for the last time, in July 2023 when he was 99½ years old and his health had become frailer. He recorded a moving video message to "my brothers, sisters, and students in Ethiopia," expressing how he never wanted to leave Ethiopia. The video is posted in the TMSAA Video Gallery.

Mr. Turenne Holding His Favorite TMSAANA Award of Gratitude Certificate, 2018

Mr. Turenne's Last Photo, June 2023

Mr. Turenne received a 100th birthday card from several alumni prior to his passing away, which he greatly appreciated. He was particularly fond of the TMSAANA Award of Gratitude Certificate he received and asked me to take one more photo of him holding it.

His funeral was held in Richelieu, Quebec, on January 13, 2024, in the presence of his adopted daughter, Mrs. Mary Turenne. His memorial service in Ethiopia was held on December 23, 2023, at the Holy Savior Catholic Church in Addis Ababa.

On February 1, 2024, TMSAA hosted "A Celebration of the Life of Mr. Roland Turenne." On the same day, TMSAA hosted the launch of the book by the Tanzanian Jesuit Rev. Festo Mkenda, SJ, titled *A Splash of Diamond: The Jesuit Presence in Ethiopia from 1945 to the Present*. Rev. Festo traveled to Addis from the Vatican for the book launch. This historical book is co-published in the Vatican and Nairobi and is adorned with many priceless historical photos, covering post-World War II Jesuit history in Ethiopia. It prominently narrates the role of Canadian Jesuits in establishing TMS and the University College of Addis Ababa (UCAA) as premier educational centers. TMSAA facilitated a group Zoom meeting for Rev. Festo with several TMS alumni, and arranged individual alumni interviews, which are reflected in the book. He kindly provided us with 120 copies of his book, which are available at TMSAA Alumni Office.

As a follow-up to Mr. Turenne's book, TMSAANA published alumnus Ermias Amare's *Memoir of a TMS Student* in 2017. Alumnus Ermias eloquently described how TMS was founded, thanks to Regent Tafari Makonnen's (later Emperor Haile Selassie's) vision that education was Ethiopia's path to joining the modern world. Education was to be the glue that would unite students from different ethnic, religious, and economic backgrounds toward a common and better future. Ermias recounts, how

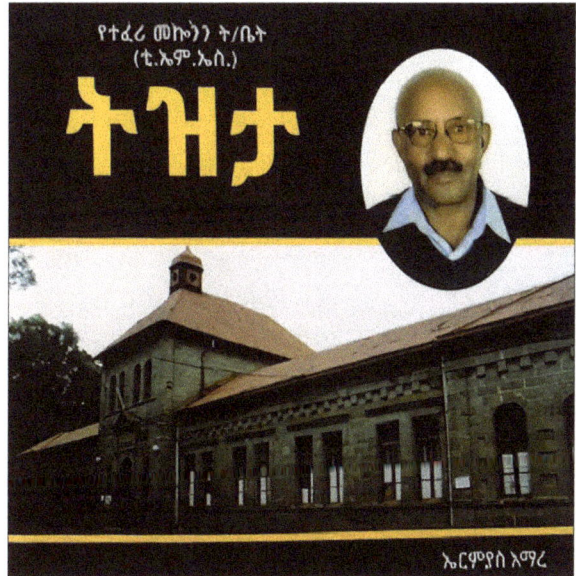

Memoir of a TMS Student by Ermias Amare

nearly all TMS students developed an almost mystic affection for their alma mater.

As he wrote in the opening chapter of his book, many mistakenly consider TMS a school for the rich and powerful due to the superior quality of education it offered, which he said cannot be further from the truth since at least 80% of the students came from families with limited income. He supports his assertion by showing a photo of his fifth-grade class, where out of 32 classmates, only one is well-dressed and has shoes, while the rest wore the simplest khaki outfits and lacked shoes. He meticulously recorded memorable recollections of past teachers and administrators, such as Ato Assefa, "the Scientist," Ato Ferisa, Sisay, and Wasihun, among others. Like Mr. Turenne's book, alumnus Ermias Amare's book ultimately became a net money maker for TMSAA.

Emahoy Tsege-Mariam Music Foundation (EMF) -TMSAA Partnership

In 2021, alumnus Temsegen Petros, TMSAA Treasurer (2014-2018), informed me that the Emahoy Tsege-Mariam Music Foundation (EMF), whose aim is to provide "access to music education for underserved children," might be able to support TMS. Since the founder and CEO of EMF, Hana Kebede, as well as the founding Board member, Daniel Assefa, were longtime acquaintances, I wrote to Daniel requesting EMF's assistance for TMS music students. Daniel informed me that even though EMF had tried without success to establish a reliable relationship with Ethiopian schools, EMF was open to assisting TMS music students. Subsequently, TMSAA, in discussion with the EPTC, prepared and submitted a proposal for funding musical instruments needed by the TMS Music Department. EMF positively responded with the first grant in 2011 and agreed to TMSAA's proposal to broaden the relationship with a long-term partnership. Starting in 2011, EMF provided the TMS Music Department, through TMSAA, with four successive grants. While the earlier grants funded the purchase of musical instruments, the 2025 grant will exclusively cover the training costs of music students.

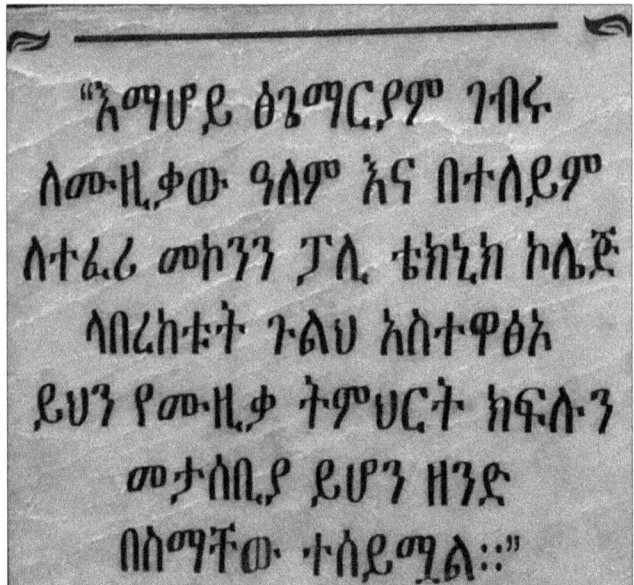

"እማሆይ ፅጌማርያም ገብሩ ለሙዚቃው ዓለም እና በተለይም ለተፈሪ መኮንን ፓሊ ቴክኒክ ኮሌጅ ላበረከቱት ጉልህ አስተዋፅኦ ይህን የሙዚቃ ትምህርት ክፍሉን መታሰቢያ ይሆን ዘንድ በስማቸው ተሰይሟል::"

Emahoy Tsege-Mariam's Bust and Plaque at the TMS Emahoy Tsege-Mariam Music Hall

In appreciation of EMF's support, TMSAA and the College were planning to honor Emahoy Tsege-Mariam on her centennial birthday on 19 December 2023. Unfortunately, she passed away on 26 March 2023 at the age of 99. To honor her lifetime of musical work and her inspiring influence on young pianists in Ethiopia and musicians worldwide, the College named the TMS Music Department after her. A bust was created by a student at the College and is now placed at the entrance of the Music Department.

TMSAA Board of Directors

I will conclude my section with a discussion of the major risk facing TMSAA from the perspective of Board governance. However, I will first highlight the following good Board practices TMSAA has developed over the years and confirm TMSAA has well-organized and well-oiled operational systems and procedures in place.

Let me start with the most important one, financial accountability and transparency. Thanks to both our past Treasurer, Temesgen Petros and our current Treasurer, Merafe Seyoum, TMSAA has a solid accountable and transparent financial management system that allows TMSAA to receive, record and report our finance with full compliance of the IRS requirements as a 501(c) (3) non-profit organization. The importance of complying with applicable legal requirements, as seen with the short life of TMSCA, cannot be emphasized enough. In addition, TMSAA uses Stripe as our payment processing platform that allows us to accept a variety of payment methods, including Credit and Debit cards, Bank Transfers and Mobile Zelle transfers, which are automatically shown on TMSAA website for specified purposes, including Membership, General Donation, Food Sharing, TMS Centennial, and more.

TMSAA Board's best-practice alumni services, include the following:

- Welcoming new alumni: with each new alumnus receiving information about TMSAA and its various activities and which TMSAA Chapter is available for joining.

- Acknowledging membership or other payments on time with an official TMSAA letter.

- On behalf of TMSAA alumni and Board, extending condolences to alumni during times of immediate family bereavement.

- Sending periodic Board Updates to alumni, which used to be quarterly but is now biannual due to the TMSAA WhatsApp that has become the main forum for TMS alumni to get news and exchange views about TMS and TMSAA.

TMSAA's inability to get alumni to volunteer to join the TMSAA Board and the lack of an effective succession plan are the most serious risk factors for the orderly continuation of TMSAA and for sustaining its accomplishments. Only with the expansion of the Board from five to nine members in April 2022, when TMSAA was re-established as a single global alumni organization, did four alumni from Ethiopia join the new expanded Board. As shown in Table 10, the earlier four Board members have been on the Board since 2012 or 2014.

Table 10: Years of Service of TMSAA Board of Directors

Board Member	Function	Alumnus Year	Years on Board	Board Term
Bisrat Aklilu	President	1967	11	2014-2025
Alem W. Hawariat	Vice President	1970	13	2012-2025
Merafe Seyoum	Treasurer	1968	7	2018-2025
Garedew Atnafseged	Member (Secretary 2014-2022)	1968	11	2014-2025
Selam Yisma	Member	1971	11	2014-2025
Debebe Eshetu	Member	1957	3	2022-2025
Tsigereda Tafesse	Secretary	1995	2	2022-2024

Table 10: Years of Service of TMSAA Board of Directors

Board Member	Function	Alumnus Year	Years on Board	Board Term
Konjit Tedla	Secretary	1973	Since 2024	2024-2025
Kebede Woldestadik	Member	1970	3	2022-2025
Lulseged Retta	Member	1970	3	2022-2025

Among the new Board members who joined in 2022 was Mrs. Tsigereda Tafesse. She served as Board Secretary and made significant contributions to the establishment of TMSAA/ Ethiopia. She had to leave the Board at the end of 2024 due to her heavy work commitments. TMSAA is fortunate Mrs. Konjit Tedla, who had held various senior positions at Ethiopian Airlines, agreed to join the Board and was appointed as Board Secretary and TMSAA Ethiopia Representative as of January 2024.

Convinced of the need for regular rotation of Board members, I had repeatedly called alumni through the many Board Updates and during the various General Assembly meetings to volunteer for Board membership or nominate others. Unfortunately, these pleas did not yield any positive result. Successive Board Election Nominating Committees, made up of alumni Bayou Tadesse, Berhan Dargie, Dr. Moges Gebremariam, and Yafet Tekele, also tried to find alumni who are willing to be considered for Board membership. Despite their concerted efforts, no alumni were willing to serve on the Board. As a result, the current Board reluctantly agreed to repeated requests to extend its term.

It is interesting how in 2018 three alumni, Abebe Abraham, Solomon Gebreab and Daniel Atnafu, recognizing the lack of alumni response to the Board's repeated call to volunteer for Board service, took upon themselves and undertook an alumni survey. They wanted to find out why alumni are hesitant to join the Board and identify and recruit members willing to join the Board. After six weeks of continuous effort, they were unable to find a single alumnus who was willing to serve on the Board. The most frequently cited reasons that alumni were not willing to join are these: health and family concerns; issues relating to old age; current commitments; fear of new commitments; workload; frequent travels within the US and abroad; and fear of disappointment. On the positive side, the survey reinforced "the fact that most who responded professed enduring love for TMS, and unqualified support to the association's success while expressing reluctance for active participation. This offers some optimism."

Recognizing the important tasks the Board is currently undertaking for the TMS name restoration and the TMS Centennial celebration, it decided to postpone replacement of the four long-serving Board members (President, Vice-President and two members) until after the TMS Centennial Celebration of 27 April 2025.

Though a TMSAA Board Election Nominating Committee will again be formed to recruit potential Board candidates, this time we will also use the 13 TMSAA Chapters network to nominate alumni candidates to be screened by the Board Election Nominating Committee. Board recruitments are normally done based on a job description and candidate competency requirements. In the case of TMSAA, it is unlikely to be used since such a process will further discourage the already reluctant alumni from offering their services.

Need for Board Orientation and Training Program

Once new Board members are elected, I strongly recommend that TMSAA adopt the standard practice of other Boards by organizing a formal TMSAA Board orientation program for the new Board members. In all the Boards I have served on, new Board members are given thorough briefings and training on the key aspects of Board members' governance responsibilities, including fiduciary and accountability issues and strategic directions focusing on the organization's specific and program development issues. In the case of TMSAA, the key issues would include membership development and program support issues. For such training, an independent Board-savvy expert should be engaged to work along with past Board members who can be resource people and share their experiences.

Need for a TMSAA Advisory Board

The TMSAA Board should consider creating an Advisory Board composed of volunteer alumni that can provide the TMSAA Board with expertise and insights that would support its decision-making. Unlike the TMSAA Board, the Advisory Board will not have any governing or fiduciary responsibilities. Their role will solely be to offer specialized advice and recommendations to the TMSAA Board.

The Advisory Board should have a clear Terms of Reference that details the expertise and experience potential members should have; the process for selecting and appointing members; the duration of the Board's service; and its meeting and reporting responsibilities to the TMSAA Board.

By setting up a TMSAA Advisory Board, the TMSAA Board can use the knowledge and skills of its alumni while keeping clear boundaries about authority and responsibility.

Appendix 1
First TMSAA Global General Assembly
Zoom Meeting Agenda

JUNE 4, 2022, 7-9 am PT; 10-12 pm EST;
4-6 pm CET; 5-7 pm Addis Ababa
TMSAA Zoom starts 9:30 am EST,
4:30 pm Addis Ababa time
Tour of TMSAA website, TMS videos,
TMSAA Activities, Music, …etc.

Opening of TMSAA General Assembly (all times below in EST)

10:00-10:10 am, Welcome and introduction of TMSAA Board, Bisrat Aklilu, President;

10:10-10:15 am, TMSAA Financials, Mrs. Merafe Seyoum, Treasurer;

10:15-10:20 am, TMSAA in Ethiopia, Artist Debebe Eshetu; Board member;

TMSAA Special Guests of Honor

10:20-10:25 am, "Mr." Roland Turenne, TMS Teacher service in Ethiopia;

10:30-10:35 am, Dr. Aklilu Habte, TMS Alumnus and Haile Selassie I University President;

10:35-10:40 am, Mr. Doug Eadie, TMS Peace Corps Teacher, 1965-1968;

TMS and TMSAA Cooperation Program

10:40-10:45 am, Dean Teshome Feissa, Entoto Polytechnic College (TMS);

10:45-10:50 am, TMSAA Future Program of Support, Alem W/Hawariat, Vice-President;

10:50-11:05 am, Questions and comments from Alumni (10 minutes)

11:05-11:25 am, TMS Alumni Voices (1 minute remarks each)
Ambassador Imru Zelleke, Virginia, USA; most senior TMS alumnus (99 years life!);
Mr. Petros Aklilu, TMSAANA Founding Board President, New Jersey, USA;

Mr. Getachew Tessema, President, former TMSACA Board, Addis Ababa, Ethiopia;

Major Argaw Kabtamu, Addis Ababa, Ethiopia;

Dr. Moges Gebremariam, Maryland, USA;

Mr. Shewangizaw Agonafer, San Diego, California, USA;
Engineer Gedion Asfaw, Addis Ababa, Ethiopia;

Mrs. Tsigereda Tafesse, Addis Ababa, Ethiopia (ECAVS/TMS)

Dr. Fantu Cheru, Stockholm, Sweden;

Mr. Dejene Tezera, Vienna, Austria;

Mr. Essayias Lisanework, Virginia, USA, (ETVTS/TMS);

Mr. Fekade Selassie Bezuneh, Atlanta, Georgia, USA;

Mr. Fisseha Tekie, Johannesburg, South Africa;

Mr. Takele Haile, Virginia, USA, (ECAVS/TMS);

Mr. Fikre Mariam Tsehay, Vancouver, Canada;

Mrs. Meaza Bekele Wegayehu, Virginia, USA;

Mr. Shewangizaw Teshome, Germany;

Mr. Yitayew Negusie, Addis Ababa, Ethiopia (TMSAA Liaison Officer);

Messrs. Bayou Tadesse & Berhane Dargie, TMSAA Board Election Committee members, New York & Washington DC, USA;

Dr. Ayele Mekruia, Addis Ababa, Ethiopia;

11:25-11:50 am Sugestions, Questions and Comments from Alumni \11:50-12:00 pm Closing Remarks and Singing of "WE ARE THE VOICE OF TAFARI MAKONNEN"

Appendix 2
Second TMSAA Global General Assembly
Zoom Meeting Agenda (times shown in EST)

1. Welcome, Alem W/Hawariat, Vice-President, TMSAA Board of Directors: 11:00 - 11:05 am

2. The State of TMSAA, Bisrat Aklilu, President, TMSAA Board of Directors: 11:10 - 11:20 am;

3. TMSAA Finances, Merafe Seyoum, Treasurer, 11:20 - 11:25 am

4. Highlights of the TMS Centennial Celebration: Dean Teshome Feissa, 11:25 - 11:35 am

5. Reports (5 to 10 mins) by the 11 TMSAA Chapter TMS Centennial Committees (TMSCCs) 11:35 am to 1:00 pm, covering:

    a) Chapter's current/potential number, 2024 membership payment, & outreach activities;

    b) Comments on the TMS Centennial Project document, and,

    c) The Chapter's proposals to support the TMS Centennial Fundraising;

        1. Canada Chapter . . . . 11:35 - 11:45 am

        2. Ethiopia Chapter . . . . 11:45 - 11:55 am

        3. Europe Chapter . . . . 11:55 - 12:05 pm

        4. Southern Africa . . . . 12:05 - 12:10 pm

        5. Middle East Chapter . . . . 12:10 - 12:15 pm

        6. USA DMV (Wash DC/Maryland/Virginia Chapter
        . . . . 12:15 - 12:25 pm

        7. USA Georgia Chapter . . . . 12:25 - 12:30 pm

        8. USA Tetra-State (Conn/Mass/NJ/NY/) Chapter
        . . . . 12:30 - 12:40 pm

        9. USA North California Chapter . . . . . . 12:40 - 12:45 pm

        10. USA South California Chapter . . . . . 12:45 - 12:55 pm

        11. USA Texas Chapter . . . . .12:55 - 1:05 pm

6. Alumni and Board members comments and questions: 20 mins, 1:05 — 1:25 pm

7. Closing Remarks and Singing of "We are the voice of TMS", 1:30 pm.

Appendix 3
Message of Mr. Getachew Tessema, Chair of Tafari Makonnen School Alumni Charity Association (TMSCA)

Founding Board of Directors, delivered to the
Third TMSAANA General Assembly, on 18 May 2016

We are impressed with TMSAANA's achievements in this short period of time, especially when we compare it to ours. Your officers have played vital role in injecting our lethargic bodies with energy and enthusiasm, to the extent that we, at times, wondered if they were contemplating a hostile takeover or a bloodless coup!

On our side, things have not been moving as fast as they should, but we are making progress. Under the bludgeoning of bureaucratic hurdles, our spirits and hopes might be low but not quite shattered — we will cross the finish line even if we have to do it worn and haggard. However, we would like to list a few of the tasks we have accomplished so far:

- Obtained the license for TMSACA.

- Prepared the website layout for TMSACA.

- Compiled a computerized list of alumni, which will be included on the website.

- Helped in the preparation and implementation of the events for TMS 90th Anniversary, i.e., layout and editing of the magazine. Collected contribution from former students and well-established organizations, which were mostly managed by former TMS students.

- Requested funding from the Canadian Embassy in Ethiopia for publication of Father Turenne's book. Unfortunately, the request was not approved. However, we have partnered with TMSAANA as you have agreed to cover the cost of printing.

- Prepared a Ten-year Development Plan for Entoto Polytechnic College as our aim is to give a better standard of education to the students.

- Made relentless effort to obtain an office in the primary TMS building known as the "Church." Unfortunately, our request did not receive a positive reply from the College.

- We are still pursuing our dream to restore TMS's name.

Finally, we would like to say that we have established a good working relationship with TMSAANA and have mapped areas of cooperation, which we hope will make our mutual desire to help our alma mater become a reputable institution a reality. To this effect, the spirit and provisions of the TMSACA-TMSAANA Memorandum of Understanding that we signed recently have guided our close collaboration to date.

I would like to finish by saying, as good old Louis-Philippe Provost (the third Canadian Jesuit TMS Director) would have put it, "Continue on the "ጥሩ መንገድ" ("the good road") on which you were "በፊት" ("before").

God bless you and TMS — and her alumni.

Afterword

Whither the Tafari Makonnen School Alumni Association?

Abebe Abraham Joteh, Contributor

TMS Class of 1968

Founder, President & CEO, CMI Management

(1986-2024)

Afterword

Introduction

Before the formation of TMSAA, my wife and I had completed our MBAs, planning to return home to start a coffee export business. However, political turmoil disrupted our plans and left us anxious and disconnected. Hoping to find a cultural connection, we moved from the Midwest to the Washington, DC, area, home to a large Ethiopian community. Yet, despite fulfilling our academic goals, we still felt lost — you have heard the expression, "all dressed up and nowhere to go!"

Amid this uncertainty, I was invited to an alumni dinner, led by our founding president, Petros Aklilu, where the need to establish an alumni association was discussed. I shortly joined as an early member and long-time supporter, primarily working behind the scenes. In my business book *Thinking Your Way Out of the Ditch*, based on proven personal experience in growing our own family business, I emphasized the value of networking with the advice: "Eat and drink with others — never alone." The message was to emphasize the importance of networking. TMSAA provides an excellent platform to build connections, networking opportunities, and foster a sense of belonging.

TMSAA

The members of the Tafari Makonnen School Alumni Association (TMSAA) are united by a shared commitment to the prosperity and legacy of our beloved Alma Mater. Bound by the principles instilled in us by the school's founder, we strive to honor the tradition of *Adera* — a dedication to education and service that has shaped our lives and continues to inspire our actions.

Through years marked by triumphs and trials, joys and hardships, we've become a community dedicated to giving back. As you read through these pages, we invite you to reflect on how you, too, can be part of something larger than yourself. By joining us in advancing the vision of Tafari Makonnen School, you'll not only contribute to a cause that will impact generations to come, but you'll also gain a sense of purpose, fulfillment, and connection. Together, we can make a lasting difference — and as you do, you'll find that your involvement enriches your own life in ways you may never have imagined.

Our Gratitude

As we begin this journey, we extend heartfelt gratitude to the TMSAA Board, the Steering Committee for this Centennial publication, and the contributing authors whose dedication and tireless efforts made this book possible. Great leaders inspire, guide, and empower others, often without due recognition. The success of any organization depends heavily on its leadership, and TMSAA has thrived under the exceptional guidance of Dr. Bisrat Aklilu, who has served as president for the past decade and contributed significantly to this effort. Special appreciation also goes to Alem Mathias, long-time Board Vice President, contributing editor, and coordinator of this writing endeavor, and finally we cannot place enough accolades on Doug Eadie, President & CEO of Doug Eadie & Company, former Peace Corps Volunteer, English and history teacher at TMS (1964 — 1967), and contributing author on this project. Doug's unwavering support and insightful *Entwined Lives* blog have greatly enriched TMSAA's forward journey. (*"Our beloved teacher! Remember this and forget it not: 'If the students have learned, it is because the teacher has taught.' You are that teacher!"*)

Highlights

In Chapter One, "TMS: An Educational Beacon for Ethiopia and the World," Doug Eadie has drawn on fifty alumni interviews, including the inspiring story of alumnus Emmanuel Abraham, to examine the keys to TMS's phenomenal success as a world-class educational institution.

Mission

The primary mission of the Tafari Makonnen School Alumni Association (TMSAA) is to connect alumni with their Alma Mater, fostering a strong network of graduates who actively engage with the school and its current students. Through events, online platforms, and community initiatives, members can expand their professional connections nationally and internationally, while also giving back through mentorship and career guidance.

Since its establishment, Tafari Makonnen School (TMS) has been fortunate to benefit from highly qualified local and foreign educators, well-equipped educational infrastructure — including teaching facilities, dormitories, and sports amenities — and a variety of extracurricular activities, all underpinned by a curriculum rooted in strong ethical discipline. These elements have prepared generations of students to serve their country and excel globally in academia, public and private sectors, and international organizations.

At the core of TMSAA is the tradition of *Adera* (solemn plea) — a commitment to safeguarding what we cherish and passing it on to future generations. This sense of duty reflects the school's enduring legacy, ensuring that the opportunities that shaped our lives remain accessible to those who follow. *Adera* is more than a tradition; it is a profound commitment to continuity and progress. Through initiatives such as scholarships and infrastructure projects, TMSAA has embraced this mission, supporting both the school and its students. These contributions uphold the high standards of education that prepare TMS students to thrive in a rapidly changing world.

For alumni, honoring *Adera* is both an obligation and a privilege — a way to give back to the institution that played a transformative role in their lives and to ensure its lasting impact for generations to come.

United by a deep appreciation for the exceptional education, ethical discipline, and extracurricular opportunities provided at TMS, we aim to create impactful contributions to the school and its community. The stories shared in this book illustrate the profound impact of this legacy.

Message for the Reader

TMSAA invites you to join our vibrant alumni network, offering opportunities to connect with professionals globally, stay informed, and grow both personally and professionally. Since its inception, Tafari Makonnen School (TMS) has empowered alumni to excel in diverse fields worldwide through its exceptional educators, facilities, and values-driven curriculum. By becoming a member of TMSAA, you'll help carry forward this legacy while building meaningful connections and accessing opportunities to thrive in an ever-changing world.

By joining TMSAA, you have the opportunity to connect, grow, and contribute. Whether through networking events, mentorship programs, or collaborative initiatives, membership in TMSAA offers a chance to enhance your personal and professional journey while ensuring the school's legacy endures. Together, we can continue this journey of service and growth, embracing the future while honoring the past.

The Centennial Celebration

As we celebrate the centennial milestone of Tafari Makonnen School (TMS), we honor a legacy of world-class education, leadership, integrity, and service that has shaped generations of students into global contributors. This historic occasion reflects on past achievements while embracing a forward-looking vision for the future.

TMS's enduring impact lies in its commitment to excellence and the dedication of its alumni, whose mentorship, networking, and philanthropy drive the school's continued success. The Tafari Makonnen School Alumni Association (TMSAA) plays a vital role in preserving this legacy, fostering connections among alumni, and supporting the school's mission.

Looking ahead, TMS is well-positioned to meet the challenges and opportunities of the next century. Its unwavering commitment to growth and its vibrant alumni network ensure that the values and traditions of TMS will continue to thrive, empowering future generations to excel and make a difference.

Keeping in Touch with the Alma Mater

When engaging with the school, it's essential to keep the conversation focused on the practical aspects of its ongoing operations. Only then can the communication provide meaningful value.

- The Tafari Makonnen School Alumni Association (TMSAA) supports TMS by staying connected with our Alma Mater and advising on resource optimization. While government funding covers the budget, we focus on helping TMS grow into a self-sustaining institution.

- Key priorities for TMS include adapting to the global workforce by equipping students with critical skills alongside academic knowledge. Building on TMS's legacy of innovation, we aim to prepare students for a dynamic, interconnected future.

- A proposal to restore the original name, Tafari Makonnen School (TMS), seeks to leverage its historical recognition, attract greater philanthropic support, and position the school as a distinguished institution. We envision TMS as a Center of Excellence, blending academic rigor with affordability to enhance its reputation and pride among stakeholders.

- Strategic initiatives include forging partnerships to ensure programs remain relevant and competitive, investing in state-of-the-art facilities for technical education, and prioritizing professional development for staff to foster a motivated and dynamic environment.

- Looking ahead, the administration envisions transforming TMS into a technical university or arts college, expanding its programs and reputation in higher education. TMSAA remains dedicated to guiding this vision and ensuring the school's continued relevance and success.

Strategic Growth Opportunities:

Leveraging the proven skills and talents of its members, TMSAA is committed to engaging in:

1. Expanding and diversifying TMSAA's mission and impact.

2. Strengthening TMSAA's governance and management systems.

3. Addressing challenges related to capitalizing on these opportunities.

The strength of any institution lies not only in its history but in the commitment of its community to its future. By uniting as a network of dedicated alumni, we can ensure TMS remains a beacon of excellence for generations to come. Let this centennial celebration be a moment for reflection and action in support of the school that has shaped us.

Alumni and the Future

TMSAA plays a critical role in sustaining the school's legacy. By offering platforms for mentorship, networking, and philanthropy, the association bridges the past and future, empowering alumni while enhancing the school's global standing. Strategic initiatives include exploring opportunities to expand TMSAA's mission, strengthening governance, and addressing challenges that come with growth. Additionally, restoring the school's original name could further bolster its historical recognition and attract greater support.

Despite all the effort you've invested in preparing yourself, earning your diploma, and feeling ready to take on the world, the job you've worked so hard for may still seem elusive. So, how can you find it? To explore how you can unlock new opportunities, follow me to the Red Sea Shore!

No doubt you have been hearing about the proposed bridge between Yemen and Djibouti, designed to accommodate over 50,000 daily travelers, representing a groundbreaking opportunity to transform regional trade, connectivity, and cross-border interactions. Beyond easing maritime congestion, this ambitious project promises to foster commerce, tourism, and employment on an unprecedented scale.

As we envision the logistics, key questions arise:

- Where will these travelers stay?
- What will they eat?
- How will they move between destinations?
- What are the opportunities present in each of these scenarios?

Addressing these considerations opens doors to economic opportunities not only for individuals but also for the broader region. This bridge is more than an infrastructure — it could very well be a catalyst for growth and a testament to the transformative power of innovation.

Step Forward

As we celebrate 100 years of excellence, let us honor the past and embrace the future. By uniting us as a network of committed alumni, we can ensure that TMS remains a beacon of leadership, integrity, and service for generations to come. Join us in carrying forward the legacy of Tafari Makonnen School — together, we will keep its light shining brightly.

About the Contributors

Bisrat Aklilu

Dr. Bisrat Aklilu, a 1967 graduate of Tafari Makonnen School, is cofounder and board president of the Tafari Makonnen School Alumni Association. After being awarded a BA in Economics and Political Science by Carleton College, an MS in Agricultural Economics by the University of Massachusetts, and a PhD in Economics by Boston University, Bisrat began a distinguished career in international development, holding key leadership positions with the United Nations System and, after retirement from the UN, as Board member of many international organizations.

Alem W. Mathias

A 1970 graduate of Tafari Makonnen School, Alem W. Mathias serves as vice president of the board of the Tafari Makonnen School Alumni Association. After earning her BS in Business Administration at Bowie State College, Alem began a highly successful career at the CSX Corporation, serving as Director of Political Affairs; Manager, Public Affairs & Affiliated PACs; Administrator & Treasurer, CSX Political Action Committee; and Manager, Government Relations Department. She has also established and operated a number of small businesses.

Abebe Abraham Joteh

A 1968 graduate of Tafari Makonnen School, Abebe Abraham Joteh earned a BS in Social Science at Baldwin-Wallace College and an MBA in Business Administration at Northwest Missouri State University. After serving as Merchandising/Marketing Manager at Better Homes & Gardens' Direct Marketing Division, and Vice President of Industry Services at BOMA International, Abebe founded CMI Management, where he served as President & CEO for thirty-eight years. Several national publications, including *The Washington Business Journal,* recognized CMI Management as among the Top 100 Largest Private Companies in its category.

Doug Eadie

Doug Eadie taught at Tafari Makonnen School as a Peace Corps Volunteer from 1964 to 1967. After earning his BA from the University of Illinois at Urbana-Champaign and his MS in Management from Case Western Reserve University, Doug held a number of executive positions in the nonprofit sector, including chief operating officer of a social services agency and vice president of a three-campus community college. Founder and president/CEO of Doug Eadie & Company, Doug is the author of 23 books on chief executive leadership and governance.

www.ingramcontent.com/pod-product-compliance
Lightning Source LLC
Chambersburg PA
CBHW041609260326
41914CB00012B/1439